Herb
Gardening
for the
Midwest

Debra Knapke
Laura Peters

LONE
PINE

Lone Pine Publishing International

The Distributor: Lone Pine Publishing
1808 B Street NW, Suite 140
Auburn, WA, USA 98001

Website: www.lonepinepublishing.com

Publisher's Cataloging-In-Publication Data
(Prepared by The Donohue Group, Inc.)

Knapke, Deb.
  Herb gardening for the Midwest / Deb Knapke, Laura Peters.

  p. : ill. ; cm.

  Includes index.
  ISBN-13: 978-976-8200-38-9
  ISBN-10: 976-8200-38-3

1. Herb gardening—Middle West. 2. Herbs—Middle West. I. Peters, Laura, 1968- II. Title.

SB351.H5 K53 2008
635/.7/0977

Photography: All studio photographs by Nanette Samol; outdoor photographs by Laura Peters, except as noted on page 256.

The Cold Hardiness Zone Map on p. 10 was adapted from the *USDA Plant Hardiness Zones Map,* found on the website of the United States National Arboretum, http://www.usna.usda.gov/Hardzone/index.html.

No plant or plant extract should be consumed unless you are certain of its identity and toxicity and of your own potential for allergic reactions. This book is not a "how-to" guide for self-medicating with herbs, and herbs should always be used with caution and the advice of trained experts.

PC: P15

Table of Contents

Introduction

What is a Herb?

This book is about herbs that have culinary, cosmetic and craft uses. You might recognize some of these uses, while others may be new to you. If you share my curiosity about plants in general, I'm confident that you'll find the 60 or so species of herbs featured here interesting enough to experiment with, regardless of your cooking or crafting expertise.

Thousands of plants have medicinal properties that have been integral to human survival since time immorial, and their medicinal value is well established. These plants are in a wide range of pharmaceuticals, some of which are life-saving drugs. The health claims for other herbs, however, are unproven and based solely on theory or tradition. Treat all medicinal herbs with respect and caution at all times. This book mentions medicinal uses of many herbs, but they are not a recommended use and are included purely for interest, particularly when herbs might be taken internally. Always consult a medical professional before using any for medicinal purposes.

That said, it is fascinating that once upon a time, people discovered that certain plants would treat particular ailments. How did they figure this out? How many people lost their lives trying to find out whether their theories were correct? It is a sobering thought.

Types of Herbs

We hope to share the joys of herbs, their smells, tastes and everything they have to offer to the artist, crafter, cook and dreamer. Grow herbs for their beauty or for their practical uses—either way, you'll continue to learn the basics of growing herbs, using their unique attributes and enjoying everything that they have to offer.

Herbs come in all forms and some cross over from one category to the next.

Roses are an example of a woody perennial, also grown as an everlasting; rose potpourri.

Perennials

Perennials are plants that develop a persistent root and bloom once they are mature. This broad definition includes trees and shrubs, but more narrowly we refer to herbaceous perennials as perennials. Herbaceous perennials generally die back to the ground in autumn and start fresh with new shoots each spring. Some plants grouped with perennials do not die back completely, and others remain green all winter. Subshrubs such as thyme and lavender are plants that have woody bases but produce herbaceous or soft new growth that turns woody in its second season. Winter conditions vary widely across the Midwest; nevertheless, some perennials will flourish and provide you with an almost limitless selection of colors, sizes and forms.

Annuals

True annuals are plants that germinate, mature, bloom, set seed and die in one growing season. The plants we treat as annuals, or bedding plants, may be annuals, biennials or tender perennials. We plant them in the spring or summer and expect to enjoy them for just that year. Many biennials, if started early enough, will flower the year you plant them, and many plants that are perennial in warmer climates will grow and flower before they succumb to our cold winter temperatures.

Annual marigold flowers make a colorful addition to a summer salad.

Annuals are grouped into three categories based on how they tolerate cold weather: hardy, half-hardy or tender. Hardy annuals tolerate low temperatures and even frost. Half-hardy annuals tolerate a light frost but will be killed by a heavy one. These annuals, generally started early from seed indoors, can be planted out around the last-frost date. Tender annuals have no frost tolerance and suffer if the temperature drops to a few degrees above freezing. The advantage to these annuals is that they often withstand hot summer temperatures.

When planting annuals, consider their ability to tolerate an unexpected frost. The dates for last frost and first

Jasmine grown on a patio in summer and brought indoors for winter.

Trees and Shrubs

Trees and shrubs are woody perennials that live for three or more years and maintain a permanent live structure above ground all year. In cold climates, a few shrubs die back to the ground each winter. The root system, protected by soil over winter, sends up new shoots in spring, and if the shrub forms flowers on new wood it will bloom that same year. Such shrubs act like herbaceous perennials, but because they are woody in their native climates they are treated as shrubs.

A tree is generally defined as a woody plant that has a single trunk and grows greater than 15' tall, and a shrub is multi-stemmed and no taller than 15'. To complicate matters, one species may grow as a tree in favorable conditions and as a shrub in harsher sites.

Woody plants are characterized by leaf type. Deciduous plants lose all their leaves each fall or winter. Evergreen trees and shrubs do not lose their leaves in the winter and can also be needled or broad-leaved. Some plants are semi-evergreen; they are generally evergreens that in cold climates lose some or all of their leaves.

Vines and Other Herbs

Vines can be annual, perennial, tropical and woody. Vegetables produce edible seeds, roots, stems, leaves, bulbs, tubers or non-sweet fruits. Aquatic or water plants grow either in water or wet soil. Bulbs are herbs with a bulb-like base that is either at soil level or under the soil. Everlastings are grown for the purpose of drying and preserving in their natural state.

Other types of herbs include tropical plants, which are native to the tropics and often grown as houseplants in our colder climates.

frost vary greatly from state to state across the U.S. Most Minnesota gardeners, for example, can expect a chance of frost from early May to early June, while Missouri is usually frost-free by late April. Ask at your local garden center about frost expectations for your area. Protecting plants from frost is relatively simple—just cover them overnight with sheets, towels, burlap or even cardboard boxes. Don't use plastic because it doesn't retain heat or provide plants with any insulation.

Herb Garden Design

Herb gardens were once created according to very particular formal designs, but today they are based on individual interpretations and desires. Herbs can be integrated into any garden setting, or they can be grown together in an area of their own. Herbs can be planted in a vegetable garden for aesthetic purposes, to use space more efficiently or as companion plants for the benefits they provide.

Herbs can be planted in theme gardens or containers. An Italian garden, with tomatoes, peppers, garlic, oregano and basil, includes all of the ingredients necessary to enjoy a traditional Italian meal. In themed gardens, ease of harvesting is as important as the plants—it's just easier to have all of the plants together within reach.

Herbs can be blended into existing garden spaces, including mixed beds and borders made up of shrubs, perennials, annuals and more. Treat the herbs just as they would be normally, based on their preference for light, soil and space, depending on what type of plants they are. What you plan to do with the plant once it's established is also important.

Factors to Consider

Once you know which herbs to grow, ask yourself a few questions to help you decide where to plant and how many to plant. Will you require a lot of the herb? Will you need to grow several plants or only one? Is it a plant that you'd prefer to bring in for the winter for year-round use, or is your season long enough for it to produce the seed or fruit necessary for its use? Garlic for example, is only useful when planted in groups—having one bulb isn't very helpful. You may only want one tarragon plant, because it is perennial, grows vigorously and to a

Rosemary in a standard form (above), lavender topiary (below)

large size, but you may want half a dozen different basil plants.

Growing Herbs Indoors

An indoor herb garden has much to offer cooks, crafters and artists—you can harvest plants easily and not have to deal with the weather. Space and light are the only two components to consider when gardening indoors. Herbs can also be grown indoors alone as specimens, or feature plants. Herbs grown indoors tend to remain smaller than those grown outdoors or in their native habitats.

The biggest challenge to growing herbs indoors is lack of sufficient light. Herbs require at least five hours of direct sunlight. West- or south-facing windows are best, depending on light conditions. Keep the windows clean so that the light isn't diffused, place the plants as close to the windows as possible and rotate the containers weekly to give all sides of the plant maximum exposure to the light.

Remember as you pot herbs in containers to add organic matter, including compost, glacial dust, earthworm castings or bat guano, to ensure that they have nutrients to draw from while indoors. Fertilizing isn't necessary because the plants are simply maintaining themselves. If nutrient deficiencies begin to show, fertilize with dilute compost tea or a naturally derived or organic fertilizer once a month. If the plants become stretched or their color fades, relocate them to a brighter spot. Harvesting regularly or pinching new growth back will also help maintain a dense habit and keep plants tidier.

Herbs grown in containers can either be grown indoors all year long, or they can brought outdoors when the risk of frost has passed. For example, woody herbs such as rosemary or kaffir lime will appreciate growing in a container in a sunny room throughout the winter, and then being moved outdoors for the summer. The additional sunlight results in flowers, fruit and new, lush growth.

Growing Herbs Outdoors

Growing herbs outdoors is as easy as it gets. Once you've chosen the right location, there's little to do other than basic care and maintenance and, of course, the harvest. You can grow your herbs on a balcony or patio, close to the kitchen, craft room or studio, or in your raised vegetable beds. Either way, herbs require the same basic care as any other plant in your garden.

Ornamental Versus Practical

The main difference between a herb garden that has been planted strictly for ornamental purposes and one that has been planted for harvesting is ease of access. If aesthetics is your only goal, then you won't need to get at your herbs very often, except for deadheading as necessary. If you plant herbs to use for practical purposes such as cooking, however, you need easy access to them to dig them up, pick the flowers or pinch back the leaves. If you always have to struggle to get to your herbs, you'll get frustrated and won't bother using them.

Garden beds planted for harvesting should be about 3 ft wide, to allow you to reach into the bed comfortably. If you want garden beds wider than that, create several beds with paths in between them. When planting herbs specifically for cooking, put them close to your kitchen so you can harvest fresh

Most herbs can be planted in either a garden (above) or in pots (below)

Cold Hardiness Zones Map

3a	▨	-35 to -40
3b	▨	-30 to -35
4a	▨	-25 to -20
4b	▨	-20 to -25

5a	▢	-15 to -20
5b	▨	-10 to -15
6a	▢	-5 to -10
6b	▨	0 to -5

herbs conveniently, even while making a meal. Raised beds are even better, particularly if you have disabilities or are elderly, because you won't have to bend over or down to weed the beds, and you be able to reach into the bed from a sitting position if your bed has a ledge.

Cold Hardiness Zones and Microclimates

Hardiness zones vary throughout the Midwest and serve as guidelines not only when choosing, but also when deciding where to plant, your herbs. North America's cold hardiness map is divided into 11 major zones. Zone 11 is the mildest while Zone 2 is the harshest. Subzones exist as well. For example,

Columbus, Ohio is mostly zone 5b, but this can vary based on microclimates. Cold hardiness zones are based on the average minimum winter temperatures sampled over many years, but each winter can offer the gardener unexpected surprises. If you're unsure of your plant hardiness zone, ask the staff at your local garden center or a gardening savvy friend. Knowing your zone may make the difference between planting something that will survive the winter outdoors and something that won't.

The microclimate of your own garden is influenced by such conditions as the nearness of buildings, how quickly the soil drains and whether your garden is in a low, cold hollow or on top of a windswept knoll or hillside.

The Basics

With good planning and preparation, you can enjoy a low-maintenance garden. It's a good idea to choose plants that perform well with little maintenance and that are generally pest and disease free.

Low-maintenance Herbs
Arugula
Borage
Catnip
Calendula
Lavender
Mint
Parsley
Perilla
Safflower
Scented Geranium
Sorrel
Thyme

Once you know what herbs you'd like to grow in your garden, learn how best to grow them to prevent costly mistakes—plan ahead rather than correct later. Make a sketch of your garden on graph paper and include its various growing conditions to help you recognize which plants will do best where.

Plants grown in ideal conditions, or conditions close to ideal, are healthier and less prone to pests and diseases than plants growing in stressful conditions. Some plants that are considered high maintenance become low maintenance when grown in the right conditions. Do not try to make your garden match the growing conditions of the plants you like. Instead, choose plants to match your garden conditions.

Sun or Shade

Buildings, trees, fences and time of day all influence the amount of light that reaches your garden. There are four

Safflower (above), borage (below)

basic categories of light in the garden: full sun, partial shade, light shade and full shade. Knowing what light is available in your garden helps you decide where to put each plant.

Full sun locations, e.g., along a south-facing wall, receive direct sunlight all or most of the day, at least 6 hours. **Partial shade** or partial sun locations, e.g., along an east- or west-facing wall, receive direct sun for part of the day

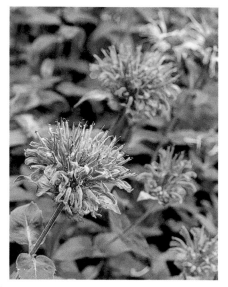

Calendula (left), bergamot (right), lemon balm (below)

and shade for the rest. **Light shade** locations receive shade most or all of the day, but some sun gets through to ground level; e.g., small dapples of sun are visible on the ground under a small-leaved tree. **Full shade** locations, e.g., the north side of a house, receive no direct sunlight.

Remember that the intensity of the full sun varies. Heat can become trapped and magnified between city buildings, baking all but the most heat-tolerant of plants in a concrete oven. Consider how long your garden is exposed to the sun. A fully exposed area can receive up to 16 hours of sunlight a day. Even a shaded northern exposure can receive a touch of sunlight in early morning and late evening. Plants that normally wouldn't burn or scorch can be affected, so provide a suitable location for touchy plant material.

Herbs for Full Sun
Basil
Bay Laurel
Borage
Calendula
Caraway
Dill
Fenugreek
Rose
Sage
Thyme

Herbs for Full to Partial Shade
Bergamot
Lemon Balm
Licorice
Lovage
Mint
Parsley
Sweet Cicely
Sweet Woodruff

Organic amendments (left to right): moisture-holding granules, earthworm castings, glacial dust, mycorrhizae, bat guano, compost, bone meal and coir fiber

Soil

Soil is the backbone of your garden, so invest in the best soil available and your plants will be amply rewarded.

Soil is made up of particles of three different sizes. Sand particles are the largest. Water drains quickly out of sandy soil and nutrients are quickly washed away. Sand has lots of air and doesn't compact easily. Clay particles are the smallest and can only be seen through a microscope. Water penetrates clay very slowly and drains very slowly. Clay holds the most nutrients, but there is very little room for air, and clay compacts quite easily. Silt is the middle-sized particle. Most soil textures are made up of a combination of these different particle sizes. These soils are called loams.

The pH is the scale on which the acidity or alkalinity of the soil is analyzed. Soils in the Midwest vary from very acidic to slightly alkaline. Most plants prefer a soil pH between 5.5 and 7.5. Soil-testing kits are available at most garden centers if you want to test your soil or check with your Cooperative Extension office to find out where your soil can be tested. Soil pH influences which nutrients are available for plants. Altering the pH of your soil can take many years and is not easy. If you want to grow only one or two plants that require a soil that is more, or less, acidic, put them in a container or raised bed to make soil pH easier to control and amend.

Another aspect to consider is how quickly the water drains out of your soil. Rocky soil on a hillside drains very quickly and should be reserved for plants that grow best in very well-drained soil. Low-lying areas tend to retain water longer, and these moist areas can be planted with herbs that require a consistent water supply. Some areas may rarely drain at all; these wet spots can be used for plants that prefer boggy conditions.

Herbs for Dry Soil
Catnip
Chives
Curry
Elderberry
Lemon Balm
Onion
Thyme

Herbs for Moist Soil
Chervil
Cress
Dill
Fennel
Fenugreek
Lemongrass
Oregano/Marjoram
Sweet Cicely

Chives (above), fenugreek (center), chicory (below)

Herbs for Sandy Soil
Anise
Chicory

Herbs for Rich Soil
Arugula
Orach

Exposure

Finally, consider the exposure in your garden. Wind, heat, cold and rain are some of the elements your garden is exposed to, and different plants are better adapted than others to the potential damage these forces can cause. Buildings, walls, fences, hills, hedges and trees can all influence your garden's exposure.

Herbs for Exposed Locations
Calendula
Dandelion
Lavender
Lemon Balm
Lemongrass
Lovage
Marigold
Mint
Safflower
Sage

Wind in particular can damage plants. Dehydration occurs in windy locations because the plants may not be able to draw water out of the soil fast enough to replace the water lost by transpiration through the leaves. Strong winds can knock down tall, stiff-stemmed perennials, and they may need to be staked in an exposed one. Use plants that are recommended for exposed sites or temper the effect of the wind with a hedge or some trees. A solid wall creates turbulence on the leeward side, while a looser structure such as a hedge breaks up the force of the wind and protects a larger area.

Preparing the Garden

Take the time before you start planting to properly prepare your garden bed—it will save time later on. First remove all weeds— the most thorough technique is to dig the bed over and pick them all out by hand—and amend the soil with organic matter.

We strongly encourage you to garden organically, particularly in your herb garden. When using plants for cooking or in creams and lotions applied to the skin or hair, it's always best to use healthy gardening practices, whether you are putting something into the soil or applying something to the plants.

Another aspect of gardening organically is using integrated pest management (IPM) to eliminate most synthesized pesticides and herbicides from your gardening regimen. Once you learn how to eliminate these toxic chemicals from your herb garden, you can do the same in your ornamental gardens. The benefits of IPM are great, and you'll find the changes subtle and easier the more frequently you put them into practice. To poison the plants, ourselves or the soil while growing them contradicts their existence completely.

That said, let us introduce you to compost, just in case you haven't met. Studies have consistently shown the benefits of gardening organically, and for the home gardener, compost truly is black gold.

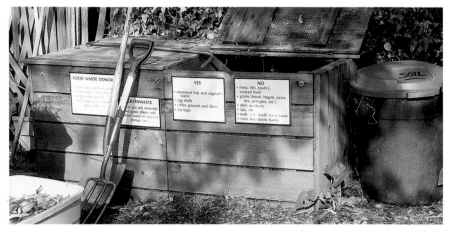

Compost

Compost is known as black gold for a reason, because organic matter benefits all kinds of soils. You can compost in a pile, wooden box or purchased composter, and the process is not complicated. A pile of kitchen scraps, grass clippings and autumn leaves will eventually break down if just left alone. Use layers of dry and fresh materials, with a higher proportion of dry matter than fresh green matter. Dry matter may be chopped straw, shredded leaves and sawdust, and green matter includes vegetable scraps and grass clippings. The smaller the pieces, the faster they will break down.

Egg shells, coffee grinds and filters, tea bags, fish bones, shrimp shells and lint from your vacuum cleaner and dryer are all beneficial additions. Do not put diseased, pest-ridden material into your compost pile—you don't want to spread problems throughout your garden. Do not add dog or cat feces, used kitty litter, fats, dairy or meat; they will attract pests and smell, resulting in a mess. Remember the basics and you'll end up with black gold.

Layer in soil or finished compost to introduce the organisms that are necessary to break down the compost pile properly. Fertilizers available at garden centers speed up the composting process. Add some water if the pile seems very dry; it needs to be moist but not soggy.

Turn the pile over or poke holes in it with a pitchfork or broom handle every week or two. Air must get into the pile to speed up decomposition.

Your compost has reached the end of its cycle when you can no longer recognize the matter that went into it and the temperature no longer rises when you turn the pile. It may take as little as a month to be ready to spread onto your garden.

A byproduct of compost is compost tea, a highly concentrated mix of organisms beneficial to the soil and ultimately to your plants. Take a piece of untreated jute or muslin, or even an old cotton pillowcase, and fill it with compost. Cinch it at the top and tie it to a wooden dowel strong enough to support it when wet. Drop the "tea bag" into a rain barrel filled with water and let it steep for a few days. Dilute this compost tea to about half, and water your plants with it. I even like to use it on my indoor plants in winter. There is no better or safer fertilizer in the world, bar none.

Planting Herbs

You can buy plants or start them from seed. Purchased plants may begin flowering the same year they are planted, but plants started from seed may take several years to mature. Starting plants from seed is more economical if you want many plants.

Plant Selection

Plants and seeds are available from garden centers, the Internet, mail-order catalogs and friends and neighbors. Garden clubs or societies sometimes promote the exchange of traditional and unusual seeds and plants, and many public gardens sell seeds of rare plants. Regardless of where you find them, make sure the source is reliable and that the herbs are not diseased or pest-ridden.

Purchased herbs are sold in pots or bare-root, usually packed in moist peat moss or sawdust. Potted plants have probably been raised in the pot. Bare-root plants are typically dormant, although some of the previous year's growth may be evident or there may be new growth starting—sometimes the piece of root appears to have no evident growth, past or present. Both potted and bare-root forms are good buys, but you still need to ensure that you are getting a plant of the best quality.

Potted herbs come in many sizes. Plants in larger containers may take longer to establish and may experience more transplant shock. The advantage is that you'll likely have a mature plant in less time. Deciding what size pot to buy depends on budget and time available for the plant to reach maturity. In the long run, herbs are going to reach their mature size regardless of what size pot you buy, so choose what's best for you.

Select plants that seem to be a good size for the pot they are in. When tapped lightly out of the pot, the roots should be visible but not winding and twisting around the inside of the pot. The leaves should be a healthy color. If they are chewed or damaged, check carefully for insects or diseases before you buy. If the plants already show these signs, do not purchase them or the problems could spread.

A trowel, soil and fertilizer are often all you need to plant herbs.

Bare-root plants are most commonly sold through mail order, but some are available in garden centers, usually in the spring. Choose roots that are dormant (without top growth). A plant already growing may take longer to establish itself— it may have too little energy to recover after growing in the stressful conditions of a plastic bag. Once you get the herbs home, plant them as soon as possible. If you have to store them briefly, water them if they are dry and keep them in a lightly shaded spot. Try to choose an overcast day to help prevent the plants from drying, and ensure that you have enough time to complete the job. The only tool you are likely to need is a trowel.

You don't have to be conservative when arranging your herb garden— plants can be grouped in natural, informal drifts. The quickest way to space out your plants is to randomly place them on the bed, mixing colors and textures as you please. Planting a small section at a time—and not allowing the roots to dry out— is especially important if you have a large bed to plant.

If you are adding just a few herbs to accent your shrub and perennial gardens, planting in random clusters of three to five herbs adds color, interest and impact.

Combine low-growing or spreading plants with tall or bushy ones. Keep the tallest plants towards the back of the bed and smallest plants towards the front. Leave enough room for the plants to spread—they may look lonely and far apart, but they will grow in quickly.

To plant potted herbs, dig a hole about the width and depth of the pot. If the beds haven't been prepared, add a trowel full of compost to the planting hole and mix it into the garden soil before adding your plant. Remove the plant from the pot. Never pull on the stem or leaves to get a plant out of a pot. It is better to cut a difficult pot off rather than risk damaging the plant. Moisten the soil to help remove the plants from their containers. Push on the bottom of the cell or pot with your thumb to ease the plants out. If the plants were growing in an undivided tray then you will have to gently untangle the roots. If the roots are very tangled, immerse them in water and wash some of the soil away to help free the plants from one another. If you must handle the plant, hold it by a leaf to avoid crushing the stems. Remove and discard any damaged leaves or growth.

Tease a few roots out of the soil ball to get the plant growing in the right direction. If the roots have become densely wound around the inside of the pot, cut into the root mass with a sharp knife to encourage new growth.

Insert your trowel into the soil and pull it towards you, creating a wedge. Place your plant into the hole and firm the soil around the plant with your hands. It should be buried to the same level that it was at in the pot, or a little higher, to allow for the soil to settle. Fill the soil in around the roots and firm it down. Water the plant well as soon as you have planted it, and regularly until it has established itself.

If you are adding just one or two plants and do not want to prepare an entire bed, dig a hole twice as wide and deep as the root ball. Add a little peat moss for improved air circulation and water retention, and to lighten up heavy, clay-based soils. Add slow release organic amendments, such as compost or a mycorrizae-based product, to the backfill of soil that you spread around the plant.

Finally, poke the identification tags into the soil next to each plant. Next spring, the tags will help you identify each herb.

In the first month after planting, just water the herbs regularly, weed and watch for pests. It helps to spread a protective mulch around the plants. You probably won't have to fertilize in the first year. If you do want to fertilize, wait until your new plants have started healthy new growth, then apply a weak organic fertilizer.

More than one herb can grow well in the same pot.

Planting Herbs into Containers

Herbs can also be grown in planters for portable displays that can be moved about the garden. Many herbs can grow in the same container without any fresh potting soil for five or six years but with just the addition of fresh compost. Be sure to fertilize and water them more often than plants in the ground. Dig your finger deep into the soil around the plant to see if it needs water. Too much water causes root rot.

Always use a good quality potting mix or a soil mix intended for containers in your planters. Don't use garden soil because it quickly loses its structure and becomes a solid lump, preventing air, water and roots from penetrating into the soil.

Containers are exposed to baking heat in summer. The soil dries out quickly in hot weather and becomes waterlogged after a couple of rainy days. Not all plants are tough enough to survive these conditions. Some invasive herbs such as mint are good choices for containers because their spread is controlled, but they are very hardy.

Herbs in planters are also more susceptible to winter damage than plants in the garden, because sides of the container are exposed to temperature fluctuations and provide very little insulation. The container itself may crack in a deep freeze. The simplest thing to do to get planters through a tough Midwest winter is to move them to a more sheltered spot. Most perennials require some cold in the winter to flower the next year, so find a spot that is still cold, but provides some shelter. An unheated garage, enclosed porch or garden shed will offer your plants more protection than they would get sitting in the great outdoors.

Basement window wells are also good places: they are sheltered, below ground and receive some heat from the window. Wait until the soil in the pots has frozen to discourage mice from making their home in the straw and feeding on the roots, and to prevent root rot. Layer straw at the bottom of the well, sit your pots on the straw, and then cover them with more straw.

The pots themselves can be weather-proofed before you put your plants into them—doing this might also be useful for high-rise dwellers with balcony gardens. Put a layer of foam insulation or "packing peanuts" at the bottom and around the inside of the pot before you add your soil and plants, making sure that excess water can still drain freely from the container. Commercial planter insulating materials are also available at garden centers.

Finally, you can bury planters in the garden for the winter. Find an open space, dig a hole deep enough to sink the planter up to its rim. Large planters require an extensive excavation or even the use of a backhoe to dig deeply enough to fit the entire pot. Another disadvantage is that recovering the planter in the spring can be messy.

Growing Perennials as Annuals

Many herbs grown as annuals here are actually perennials or shrubs that are native to warmer climates and unable to survive our cold winters. Some tropical perennials need special treatment to help them survive winter, or can be brought inside and treated as houseplants in the colder months.

A reverse hardening-off process is used to acclimatize plants to an indoor environment. Plants such as scented geranium and heliotrope, which are grown in the sun all summer, should be gradually moved to shady garden spots. They develop more efficient leaves that are capable of surviving in the comparatively limited light indoors.

Perennial herbs with tuberous roots can be stored over winter and replanted in late winter or early spring. Dig up plants in fall after they die back but before the ground freezes. Shake the loose dirt away from the roots and let them dry out a bit in a cool, dark place. Once they are dry and clean, dust them with an anti-fungal powder (found at garden centers) and store them in moist peat moss or coarse sawdust. Keep them in a dark, dry place that is cold but doesn't freeze. Pot them if they start to sprout, and keep them in moist soil in a bright window. Pot them up by late winter or early spring whether they have already started sprouting or not, so they will be ready for spring planting.

If winter storage sounds like too much work, replace your annual herbs each year and leave the hard work to the growers.

Perennial Herbs Grown as Annuals
Curry
Marjoram
Rosemary
Vietnamese Coriander

Curry (above), oregano (center)

Vietnamese coriander (below)

Caring for Your Herbs

Many herbs require little care, but all will benefit from a few maintenance basics. Weeding, pruning, deadheading and staking are just a few of the chores that, when done regularly, minimize major work.

Weeding

Controlling weeds is one of the most important things to do in your garden. Weeds compete with herbs for light, nutrients and space. Weeds can also harbor pests and diseases. Try to prevent weeds from germinating. If they do, pull them out while they are still small before they have a chance to flower, set seed and start a whole new generation of problems.

Weeds can be pulled out by hand or with a hoe. Quickly scuffing across the soil surface with the hoe will pull out small weeds and sever larger ones from their roots. A layer of mulch is an excellent way to suppress weeds.

Mulching

Mulches prevent weed seeds from germinating by blocking out the light. Soil temperatures remain more consistent and more moisture is retained under a layer of mulch. Mulch also prevents soil erosion during heavy rain or strong winds. Organic mulches consist of such materials as compost, bark chips and shredded leaves. Organic mulches are desirable because they improve the soil and add nutrients as they break down.

In spring, spread about 2" of mulch around your plants, keeping the area immediately around their crowns or stems clear. Mulch that is too close can trap moisture and prevent good air circulation, encouraging disease. If the layer of mulch disappears into the soil over summer, replenish it.

Put a fresh layer of mulch, up to 4" thick, around the plants for winter protection once the ground freezes in fall. This mulch is particularly important if you can't depend on a steady layer of snow to cover your garden in the winter. You can cover the plants with dry material such as straw, pine needles, finely shredded bark fines or shredded leaves.

Keep in mind that as the ground freezes, so too may your pile of potential mulch. One solution is to cover most of the bed with mulch, leaving only the plants exposed, before the ground freezes. Put extra mulch, needed to cover the plants, in a large plastic bag or your wheelbarrow and put it somewhere that takes longer to freeze, perhaps the garage or garden shed. Once the ground is completely frozen, you use that mulch to cover the plants.

In late winter or early spring, once the weather starts to warm up, pull the mulch layer off the plants and see if they have started growing. If they have, you can pull the mulch back, but keep it nearby in case you need to put it back on to protect the tender new growth from a late frost. Once your plants are well on their way and you are no longer worried about frost, remove the protective mulch completely and spread it on other beds in the yard or compost it.

Deadheading

Deadheading—the removal of flowers once they are finished blooming—keeps plants looking tidy, prevents the plant from spreading seeds (and therefore seedlings) throughout the garden, often prolongs blooming and helps prevent pest and disease problems.

Deadheading is not necessary for every plant. Some plants with seedheads are left in place to provide interest in the garden over winter. Other plants are short-lived and by leaving some of the seedheads in place you encourage future generations to replace the old plants.

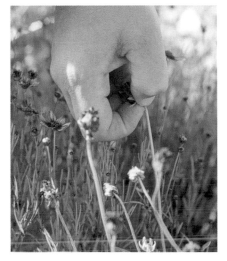

Flowers can be pinched off by hand or snipped off with hand pruners. Bushy plants that have many tiny flowers, particularly ones that have a short bloom period such as thyme, can be more aggressively pruned back with garden shears once they are done flowering. Shearing some plants such as oregano will promote new growth and possibly blooms later in the season.

Herbs Grown for their Seeds
Anise
Arugula
Basil
Caraway
Dill
Coriander
Fennel
Lovage
Nasturtium
Perilla
Safflower

Herbs that Self-seed
Arugula
Chives
Lemon Balm
Red Valerian
Salad Burnet
Sweet Cicely

Nasturtium seeds

Red valerian

Pruning

Many plants benefit from some grooming. Resilient health, plentiful blooming and more compact growth are signs of a well-groomed garden. Pinching, thinning and disbudding plants before they flower enhances the beauty of the herb garden. The methods for pruning are simple, but some experimentation is required to get the right.

Thinning is done to clump-forming plants such as bee balm early in the year when shoots have just emerged. These plants develop a clump of stems that allows very little air or light into the center of the plant. Removing half of the shoots when they first emerge will increase air circulation and prevent diseases such as powdery mildew. The increased light encourages more compact growth and more flowers. Throughout the growing season, thin any growth that is weak, diseased or growing in the wrong direction.

Trimming or pinching plants is a simple procedure, but timing it correctly and achieving just the right look can be tricky. Early in the year, before the flower buds have appeared, trim the plant to encourage new side shoots. Stem by stem, remove the tip and some stem of the plant just above a leaf or pair of leaves. If you have a lot of plants, you can trim off the tops with your hedge shears to one-third of the height you expect the plants to reach. The growth that begins to emerge can be pinched again. Beautiful layered effects can be achieved by staggering the trimming times by a week or two.

Give plants enough time to set buds and flower. Most spring-flowering plants cannot be pinched back or they will not flower. Early summer or mid-summer bloomers should be pinched only once, as early in the season as possible. Late summer and fall bloomers can be pinched several times but leave them alone past June. Don't pinch the plant if flower buds have formed—it may not have enough energy or time left in the year to develop a new set of buds. Experimentation and keeping detailed notes will improve your pinching skills.

Staking

A few plants will need some support to look their best. Plants that develop tall spikes require each spike to be staked individually. Push a strong, narrow pole such as a bamboo stake into the ground early in the year and tie the spike to the stake as it grows. A forked branch can also be used to support single-stem plants.

Many plants get top-heavy and tend to flop over once they reach a certain height. A wire hoop, sometimes called a peony ring, is the most unobtrusive way to hold up such a plant. When the plant is young, push the legs of the peony ring into the ground around it and as the plant grows up, the wire or plastic ring supports it. At the same time the bushy growth hides the ring. Wire tomato cages can also be used.

Support plants with floppy tangles of stems with twiggy branches inserted into the ground around them.

Some people consider any stakes to be unsightly. To reduce the need for staking, don't use a richer soil than is recommended—very rich soil causes many plants to produce weak, leggy growth prone to falling over. Also, a plant that likes full sun will be stretched out and leggy if grown in the shade. You can also mix in plants that have a more stable structure between the plants that need support. A floppy plant may still fall over slightly, but only as far as its neighbor will allow. Many plants are available in compact varieties that don't require staking.

Herbs that May Require Staking or Support
Bay Laurel
Dill
Hops
Hyssop
Licorice
Orach
Tarragon

Some herbs grow large enough to require staking.

Watering

Many plants need little supplemental watering if they have been planted in their preferred conditions and are given a moisture-retaining mulch. The rule of watering is to water thoroughly and infrequently, and make sure the water penetrates deeply into the soil.

Fertilizing

If you prepare your beds well and add new compost to them each spring, you should not need to add extra fertilizer. If you have a limited amount of compost, you can mix a slow-release organic fertilizer into the soil around your herbs in the spring. Some plants are heavy feeders that need additional supplements throughout the growing season.

Many organic fertilizers are available at garden centers. Always use the recommended quantity, because too much fertilizer will do more harm than good.

Propagation

Learning to propagate your own plants is an interesting and challenging aspect of gardening that can save you money, but it also takes time and space. Seeds, cuttings and divisions are the three methods of increasing your plant population. There are benefits and problems associated with each method.

Seeds

Starting herbs from seed is a great way to propagate many plants that grow easily from seed and flower within a year or two of being transplanted into the garden. You can buy seeds or collect them from your own or a friend's garden. Remember that some cultivars and varieties don't pass on their desirable traits to their offspring. Other plants take a very long time to germinate, if they germinate at all, and an even longer time to grow to flowering size.

A few basic rules exist for starting all seeds. Some seeds can be started directly in the garden, but it is easier to control temperature and moisture levels and to provide a sterile environment if you start the seeds indoors. Seeds can be started in pots or, if you need a lot of plants, in flats. Use a sterile soil mix intended for starting seeds. The soil will need to be kept moist but not soggy. Most seeds germinate in moderately warm temperatures of about 57°–70° F. Seed-starting supplies including plastic seed-tray dividers (often called plug trays) and heating coils or pads are available at garden centers.

All seedlings are susceptible to a problem called "damping off," which is caused by soil-borne fungal organisms. An afflicted seedling looks as though someone has pinched the stem at soil level, causing the plant to topple over.

Some materials for starting seeds and a prepared seed tray

The pinched area blackens and the seedling dies. Sterile soil mix, air circulation and evenly moist soil help prevent this problem. Products are also available at your local garden center to prevent damping off.

Fill your pot or seed tray with the soil mix and firm it down slightly—not too firmly or the soil will not drain—and moisten the soil thoroughly. Plant only one type of seed per pot or flat. Large seeds can be placed individually and spaced out in pots or trays. If you have divided inserts for your trays you can plant one or two seeds per section. Sprinkle small seeds more randomly. Mix tiny seeds with some very fine sand and spread on the soil surface. These tiny seeds may not need to be covered with any more soil. The medium-sized seeds can be lightly covered and the larger seeds can be pressed into the soil and then lightly covered. Do not cover seeds that need to be exposed to light in order to germinate. Water the seeds using the very fine spray of a hand-held spray bottle if the soil starts to dry out.

To keep the environment moist, place pots inside clear plastic bags. Change the bag or turn it inside out when condensation starts to build up and drip. Many seed trays come with clear plastic covers, which keep the moisture in. Remove the covers once the seeds have germinated.

Seeds generally do not require a lot of light to germinate, so pots or trays can be kept in a warm, out of the way place. Once the seeds have germinated, place them in a bright location but out of direct sun. Transplant the herbs to individual pots once they have three or four true leaves. Plants in plug trays can be left until neighboring leaves start to touch each other, then transplant them to pots.

The seed itself provides all the nutrition the seedling will need. Fertilizing causes young seedlings to produce soft, spindly growth that is susceptible to attack by insects and diseases. A fertilizer, diluted to ¼ or ½ strength, can be used once seedlings have four or five true leaves.

Many seeds will easily grow as soon as they are planted, but others need to have their defenses lowered before they will germinate. Some seeds also produce poisonous chemicals in their seed coats to deter insects. Some thick-coated seeds can be soaked for a day or two in water to promote germination, thus mimicking the end of the dry season and the start of the rainy season, which is when the plant would germinate in its natural environment. Other thick-coated seeds need to have their seed coats scratched to allow moisture to penetrate the seed coat and prompt germination. Nick the seeds with a

Grow lights (above), chamomile repels insects and fungus (below)

Cinnamon powder is a natural fungicide and has been shown to be particularly effective against damping-off. In addition, weak, cooled chamomile tea is another natural fungicide.

knife or gently rub them between two sheets of sand paper. Leave the seeds in a dry place for a day or so before planting them to give the seeds a chance to get ready for germination before they are exposed to water.

Plants from northern climates often have seeds that wait until spring before they germinate. These seeds must be given a period of cold before they will

Herbs planted in a strawberry planter

The lid lets light in and collects some heat during the day and prevents rain from damaging tender plants. If the interior gets too hot, the lid can be raised for ventilation. A hot frame is insulated and has heating coils in the floor to prevent the soil from freezing or to maintain a constant soil temperature for germinating seeds, or rooting cuttings.

Herbs to Start from Seed
Arugula
Caraway
Chervil
Dill
Marigold
Orach
Parsley
Nasturtium
Strawberry

Cuttings

Cuttings are an excellent way to propagate varieties and cultivars that you really like but that don't come true from seed or that don't produce seed at all. Each cutting will grow into a reproduction of the parent plant. Cuttings are taken from the stems of some plants and the roots of others.

Stem Cuttings

Stem cuttings are generally taken in the spring and early summer. Avoid taking cuttings from plants that are in flower—plants that are busy growing are full of the right hormones to promote quick root growth, not busy reproducing. If you do take cuttings from plants that are flowering be sure to remove the flowers and the buds to divert the plant's energy back into growing.

Cuttings need to be kept in a warm, humid place to root, which makes them very prone to fungal diseases. Providing proper sanitation and encouraging

germinate. You can put the seeds in a pot or tray in the refrigerator for up to two months, but check them regularly and don't allow them to dry out. A less space-consuming method is to mix the seeds with some moistened sand, peat or sphagnum moss in a sealable sandwich bag and pop it in the refrigerator for up to two months, again being sure the sand or moss doesn't dry. The seeds can then be planted in the pot or tray.

A cold frame can protect tender plants over the winter, start vegetable seeds early in the spring, harden plants off before moving them to the garden, protect fall-germinating seedlings and young cuttings or divisions, and start seeds that need a cold treatment. This mini-greenhouse structure is built so that ground level on the inside of the cold frame is lower than on the outside. The angled, hinged lid is fitted with glass. The soil around the outside of the cold frame insulates the plants inside.

quick rooting will increase the survival rate of your cuttings.

Debate exists over what the size of cuttings should be. A small cutting is 1–2" long and a large cutting is 4–6" long. You can try different sizes to see what works best for you. Determine the size of cuttings by the number of leaf nodes on the cutting. You will want at least three or four nodes (the node is where the leaf joins the stem, and it is from here that the new roots will grow). The base of the cutting will be just below a node. Strip the leaves gently from the first and second nodes, and plant them below the soil. The new plants will grow from the nodes above the soil. The leaves can be left in place on the cutting above ground. Sometimes there is a lot of space between nodes, so your cutting will be longer than recommended. Some plants with almost no space at all between nodes can be cut to the recommended length. Gently remove the leaves from the lower half of the cutting. Plants with several nodes close together often root quickly and abundantly.

Always use a sharp, sterile knife to make the cuttings. Cut straight across the stem. Once you have stripped the leaves, you can dip the end of the cutting into a rooting-hormone powder intended for softwood cuttings. Sprinkle the powder onto a piece of paper and dip the cuttings into it. Discard any extra powder left on the paper. Tap or blow the extra powder off the cutting. Your cuttings are now prepared for planting.

The sooner you plant your cuttings the better. Plant the cuttings the same way you would seeds, and keep in a warm place, about 65–70° F, in bright, indirect light.

Strawberry planted with yarrow

Most cuttings will require from one to four weeks to root. After two weeks, give the cutting a gentle tug. You will feel resistance if roots have formed. If the cutting feels as though it can pull out of the soil mix then gently push it back down and leave it for longer. New growth is also a good sign that your cutting has rooted. Some gardeners leave the cuttings alone until they can see roots through the holes in the bottoms of the pots. Uncover the cuttings once they have developed roots.

Apply a foliar feed when the cuttings show new leaf growth. Plants quickly absorb nutrients through the leaves; therefore, you can avoid stressing the

Left to right: trim the lower leaves of your cutting; cuttings with strong root growth are ready for potting; dip the end in rooting hormone; firm soil gently around cutting; several cuttings can grow in one pot until they show new growth

newly formed roots. Garden centers have foliar feeds and information about applying them.

Once your cuttings have rooted and have established themselves, they can be potted up individually. If you rooted several cuttings in one pot or tray, the roots may have tangled together. If gentle pulling doesn't separate them, take the entire clump and rinse some of the soil away. That should free the roots enough to separate the plants.

Pot the young plants in a sterile potting soil. Move them into a sheltered area of the garden or a cold frame and grow until they are large enough to plant in the garden. They may need some protection over the first winter. Keep them in the cold frame if they are still in pots. Give them an extra layer of mulch if they have been planted out.

Basal Cuttings

Basal cuttings involve removing the new growth from the main clump and rooting it in the same manner as stem cuttings. Many plants send up new shoots or plantlets around their bases. Often, the plantlets will already have a

few roots growing. The young plants develop quickly and may even grow to flowering size the first summer. You may have to cut back some of the top growth of the shoot because the tiny developing roots won't be able to support a lot of top growth. Treat these cuttings the same way as a stem cutting.

Root Cuttings

Dandelions are well known for foiling every attempt to eradicate them: even the smallest piece of root left in the ground can sprout a new plant. Other perennials share this trait, and the main difference between starting root cuttings and stem cuttings is that the root cuttings must be kept fairly dry because they can rot easily.

Take cuttings from the fleshy roots of certain plants in early- or mid-spring when the ground is just starting to warm up and the roots are just about to break dormancy. At this time, the roots of the plants are full of nutrients, which the plants stored the previous summer and fall, and hormones are initiating growth. Wet the soil around the plant so that you can loosen it enough to get to the roots.

Keep the roots slightly moist, but not wet, while you are rooting them, and keep track of which end is up. Roots must be planted in a vertical, not horizontal, position on the soil, and roots need to be kept in the orientation they held while previously attached to the parent plant. People use different methods to recognize the top from the bottom of the roots; some gardeners cut straight across the tops and diagonally across the bottoms.

You do not want very young or very old roots. Very young roots are usually white and quite soft; very old roots are tough and woody. The roots you should use will be tan colored and still fleshy. To prepare your root, cut out the section you will be using with a sterile knife. Cut the root into pieces that are 1–2" long. Remove any side roots before planting the sections in pots or planting trays. Use the same type of soil mix the seeds and stem cuttings were started in. Poke the pieces vertically into the soil and leave a tiny bit of the top poking up out of the soil.

Keep the pots in a warm place out of direct sunlight and don't over-water. The plants will send up new shoots once they have rooted. They can be planted in the same manner as stem cuttings (see p. 28).

Rhizomes are the easiest root cuttings with which to propagate plants. Rhizomes are thick, fleshy roots that grow horizontally along the ground, or just under the soil. Periodically, they send up new shoots from along the length of the rhizome, spreading out the plant. Take rhizome cuttings when the plant is growing vigorously (usually in the late spring or early summer).

Dig up a section of rhizome and note that it grows in sections. The places where these sections join are called nodes. It is from these nodes that feeder roots (smaller stringy roots) extend downwards and new plants sprout upwards. You may even see that small plants are already sprouting. Cut the rhizome into pieces, with a node in each piece.

Fill a pot or planting tray to about 1" from the top with perlite, vermiculite or seeding soil mix. Moisten the soil and let the excess water drain away. Lay the rhizome pieces flat on the top of the soil and almost cover them with more soil mix. If you leave a small bit of the top exposed to the light it will encourage the shoots to sprout. The soil mix does not have to be kept wet, but you should moisten it when it dries out to avoid having your rhizome rot. Once your cuttings have established themselves they can be potted individually and grow on in the same manner as the stem cuttings (see p. 28).

Oregano, thyme, rosemary, chives and flat-leaf parsley (left), hops (right)

Herbs to Propagate from Cuttings
Hops
Lemon Verbena
Mint
Oregano/Marjoram
Rosemary
Scented Geranium
Soapwort
Tarragon

Division

Division is quite possibly the easiest way to propagate plants. Annuals, perennials and most tropical plants can be divided, but trees, shrubs or any woody ornamentals, including some vines, cannot be divided because they share a central stem or crown. If that central stem or crown is divided, all of the plant will fail.

Most plants form larger and larger clumps as they grow. Dividing this clump will rejuvenate the plant, keep its size in check and provide you with more plants. How often a plant can be divided will vary. Some plants need dividing almost every year to keep

them vigorous, while others can last a few years before dividing. You will know when a perennial should be divided if:
• the center of the plant has died out
• the plant is no longer flowering as profusely as it did in previous years
• the plant is encroaching on the growing space of other plants in the bed.

Begin by digging up the entire plant and knocking any large clods of soil away from the root ball. The clump can then be split into several pieces. A small plant with fibrous roots can be torn into sections by hand. A large plant can be pried apart with a pair of garden forks inserted back to back into the clump. Plants with thicker tuberous or rhizomatous roots can be cut into sections with a sharp, sterile knife. In all cases, cut away any old sections that have died out and replant only the newer, more vigorous sections.

Once your original clump is divided into sections, replant one or two of them in the original location. Work organic matter into the soil before replanting. The other sections can be moved to new spots in the garden or potted up and given away. Get the sections back into the ground as quickly as possible to prevent the exposed roots from drying out. Put your plant divisions in pots if you aren't sure where to put them. Water new transplants thoroughly and keep them well watered until they have re-established themselves.

The larger the sections of the division, the more quickly the plant will re-establish itself and grow to blooming size again. Very small divisions may benefit from being planted in pots until they are bigger and better able to fend for themselves in the border.

Newly planted divisions will need extra care and attention when they are first planted. They will need regular watering and, for the first few days, shade from direct sunlight. A light covering of burlap or damp newspaper should be sufficient shelter for this short period. Move divisions that have been planted in pots to the shade.

Some gardeners prefer to divide plants while they are dormant, whereas others feel plants establish themselves more quickly if divided when they are growing vigorously. Experiment with dividing at different times of the year to see what works best. If you do divide plants while they are growing, you will need to cut back one-third to one-half of the growth so as not to stress the roots while they are repairing the damage done to them.

Herbs to Propagate by Division
Bee Balm
Calamint
Chamomile
Licorice
Lovage
Soapwort
Tarragon

If the plant you want to divide is not too large, a section of it can be divided off and replanted.

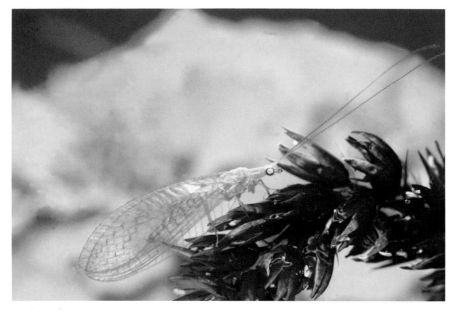

Pests and Diseases

Your garden may experience attacks from pests and diseases from time to time. There are numerous ways to deal with any problems that arise. Integrated Pest (or Plant) Management (IPM) is a moderate approach for dealing with pests and diseases. The goal of IPM is to reduce pest problems to levels of damage acceptable to you. Attempting to totally eradicate pests is futile. Consider whether a pest's damage is localized or covers the entire plant. Will the damage kill the plant, or is it only affecting the outward appearance? Can the pest be controlled without chemicals?

IPM includes learning about your plants and the conditions they need for healthy growth. It is also useful for you to learn what pests might affect your plants, where and when to look for those pests and how to control them. Keep records of pest damage because your observations can reveal patterns useful in spotting recurring problems and in planning your maintenance regime.

Prevention and Control

The first line of defence for your plants is to prevent pests and diseases from attacking in the first place. Provide the conditions necessary for healthy plant growth. Healthy plants are able to fend for themselves and can sustain some damage. Plants that are stressed or weakened are more subject to attack. Begin by choosing pest-resistant plants. Keep your soil healthy by using plenty of good-quality compost. Spray your plant's foliage with compost tea or fish emulsion, which acts as a foliar feed and also prevents fungal diseases.

Other cultural practices can help prevent pest attacks. Provide enough space for your plants so that they have good air circulation around them and are not stressed from competing for available resources. Remove plants that are decimated by pests and dispose of diseased foliage and branches. Keep your gardening tools clean and tidy up fallen leaves and dead plant matter in and around your permanently planted containers at the end of every growing season.

Physical controls are generally used to combat insect and mammal problems; for example, picking insects off plants by hand, which is easy if you catch the problem when it is just beginning. Large, slow insects are particularly easy to pick off. You can squish or rub off colonies of insects with your fingers. Other physical controls include traps, barriers, scarecrows and natural repellants that make a plant taste or smell bad to pests. Garden centers offer a wide array of such devices. Physical control of diseases usually involves removing the infected plant or parts of the plant to keep the problem from spreading.

Biological controls make use of populations of natural predators. Birds, spiders and many insects help keep pest populations at a manageable level. Encourage these creatures to take up permanent residence in or near your garden by planting appropriate food sources. Bird baths and feeders encourage birds to visit your garden and feed on a wide variety of insect pests. Many beneficial insects eat nectar from flowers.

Use chemical controls only as a last resort. Pesticide products can be either organic or synthetic. If you have tried the other suggested methods and still wish to take further action, try to use organic types, which are available at most garden centers.

Beneficial bugs: lacewing (top left), ladybug (center), ladybug larvae (below).

Chemical or organic pesticides may also kill the beneficial insects you have been attracting. Many people think that because a pesticide is organic, they can use as much as they want. An organic spray kills because it contains a lethal toxin. NEVER overuse any pesticide. When using pesticides, follow the manufacturer's instructions carefully and apply in the recommended amounts only to the pests listed on the label. A large amount of pesticide is not any more effective in controlling pests than the recommended amount.

Caraway flowers attract beneficial insects.

What Now?

The herbs are planted and thriving in your garden outside and on your windowsill indoors, and they're all ready for harvest. Herbs are grown for a variety of purposes and for their different parts—their leaves, flowers, stems, roots, seeds and fruit. Some herbs may only have one "useful" part that is great for cooking and others are useful from top to bottom. A variety of ways exist to harvest and preserve the useful parts of the plant. These processes were commonly known in the 17th century but in many ways have become a lost art. Today we can still take simple steps to use and preserve herbs.

Nasturtiums add color to salads.

The Harvest

For most herb gardeners, the delight is in the harvest. After a long season of growing, tending and care, the time finally arrives to collect the plant parts necessary to use throughout the year. Fortunately there's no magic moment when this all occurs, because most of the herbs recommended here produce leaves that are useful to the cook, artist and crafter. Leaves can be harvested all throughout the growing season, or all year-round when grown either in a climate that allows it or indoors. Flowers that are used fresh can also be picked throughout their blooming cycle.

There are no hard and fast rules when it comes to harvesting your herbs, you need to keep a few things in mind, such as when and how to pick them at their peak. First, depending on the size of the plant and how much lush growth is produced, pinch out growth for use on a regular basis. Don't take too much at a time: you will have to wait longer between harvests if you take more than 30–50 percent of the plant at once during the growing season. If a hard shearing is necessary to perk up the plant, go ahead—it won't hurt the plant's longevity. The plant will only reproduce what was taken away, time and energy allowing. If the growing season has come to an end, then you may want to cut the plant back to the base.

Pinching out the tips of branched plants encourages new growth as well as a bushier, denser growth habit. It can also enable the plant to divert some of its energy to other portions of the plant: for example, energy and nutrient storage in the roots, rhizomes or bulbs; flower, fruit and seed production; preparation for dormancy and awakening in the spring, and the production of the essential oils in every part of the plant.

The best time to harvest is when a plant's oil content is at its maximum. For most leafy herbs, this time is when the plant's flowers are just about to open. Mint is of one of the exceptions because the oils are at their maximum when the flowers are open completely. Usually seeds are harvested once they've turned color, often from green to brown, usually in the fall. Seeds should be harvested before they fall to the ground, but only because it is much easier than trying to pick them out of the soil, and before they begin to germinate. Roots are mostly harvested in the fall, once the growing season is finished. At this point, they're often fully developed and their storage is filled to capacity. Flowers vary somewhat as to when they should be harvested. For example, chamomile flowers should be picked when they're fully open. Some are better harvested just before they open while others are best picked just after they've opened.

To harvest herbs throughout the growing season, make sure you have

Chopped curly-leaf parsley

sharp tools because dull blades may damage the plant or cause injuries to you. Pinch leaves from the tenderest parts of the plant, avoiding the woody portions, unless you plan on discarding them in the long run.

Morning is always the best time to harvest. Wait until the dew has evaporated but before it gets too hot. It's important to preserve the essential oils, and the hottest part of the day is when they're at their lowest. Remember the general rule: if the leaf is safe to eat then the flowers are as well. If the plant is in the midst of a blooming cycle, you may want to pick some of the flowers along with the leaves, for immediate or later use. Ideally, waiting an average of one two days after a thorough watering is also best, so the leaves are plump and bursting with essential oils. Place the stems in a little water and refrigerate for a few hours before cleaning and processing for storage, especially long term.

Herbs grown particularly for their edible flowers, such as nasturtiums, should only be picked immediately before you plan on preparing the meal. Freshly picked flowers don't store well and their flavors are at their best in early morning and late afternoon when the volatile oils are at their most concentrated. Rinse the flowers gently under tepid water, just as you would rinse the leaves, to remove any dirty residue or insects that may be tucked away. The flowers can also be soaked in water with a small amount of salt for about 15 minutes to ensure they're clean. Dry the flowers with a soft, dry towel or paper towel and refrigerate until needed. If you must cut the flowers several hours before serving them, treat them as you would fresh flowers for a bouquet. Keep the flowers on their stems and the stems in water, and refrigerate them until needed.

A bumper crop of onions!

Collecting seeds is probably one of the easiest and fun parts of the harvest. Some seeds come encapsulated in a cover or remain on the inside the fruit, preventing the ripened seeds from escaping and falling to the ground. For plants with seeds that spill all over the ground once they've ripened, collect them before they drop. To prevent their escape, place a small, brown paper bag over the seed head shortly before the seeds ripen and turn brown to reddish brown, if not black. Gently cinch the mouth of the bag to the stem without cutting into the stem. Once the seeds have ripened and dried, cut the stem where the bag is attached and shake freely into the bag. If the seeds require a drying period, they can also be dried in the bag and stored in an airtight container later.

Harvesting roots is as simple as digging them up, and usually at the end of the season, particularly with annuals or plants grown as annuals. Remove the entire root of annuals when you're doing your fall clean-up. For hardy plants that you intend to leave in the ground, such as shrubs and perennials, remove only a part of the root and leave the rest. Remove no more than approximately one-third of the root to prevent shock to the plant. It will need at least two-thirds of the root to support the rest of the plant the following year. Gently rinse the soil from the root and let it dry for further processing. Don't be tempted to brush the soil from the root with a brush, because even the softest of bristles can damage the tender tissues you've so carefully grown.

Bulbs, such as onions and garlic, should be dug up either in late summer or early fall, depending on when you planted them.

Potpourris with mint (left) and rose petals (right)

Processing and Preservation

One of the wonderful things about herbs is that so many can be dried, frozen or preserved in some way for later use. Each method is simple, and you'll be out in your garden harvesting, collecting and preserving your herbs in no time.

Drying Herbs

Drying herbs is probably the most common form of home preserving. It is important to ensure that all of the moisture is removed from the fresh leaves. A location with adequate to excellent air circulation is imperative, as is enough space to dry the herbs themselves. If mold sets in because the humidity is too high, the fresh material is still too wet. If the air is does not circulate, then your herbs are doomed. An average temperature to dry herbs at home is 68–90°F. To preserve the color of your herbs, dry them in a dark place

You can dry herbs in the oven, particularly if you want to speed up the process. Most ovens are too hot to dry flowers and leaves even on their lowest settings, but they are well suited to drying roots. The microwave is another option for drying herbs but it's tricky because the heat causes the herbs to arc. To lessen this problem, place a small dish of water next to the herbs to boost the humidity— but the humidity can counteract drying herbs. Dehydrators are wonderful for drying leaves, flowers, fruit and seeds. Athough they can be expensive, a dehydrator is one of the best investments you can make if you plan to dry a lot of herbs over the years.

Air-drying is the easiest, least labour intensive and most successful process. Small-leaved green herbs can be left on their stems for drying, and larger-leaved herbs can be gently separated from the stems and left to dry spread out on screens, fabric or trays. Most gardeners collect a handful of leafy stems, tie their stems together in a bunch and hang them upside down until dry. This way is perfect for drying your leafy stems and flowers. Drying racks, whether they're

Chive flower

if they fall and to prevent them from getting dusty.

Depending on what you're using the flowers for, they can either be left intact once dry or stripped from their stems just as you would with the leaves. Some of the flowers can be dried upright, such as rosebuds and chive flowers. They're really only useful for decorative purposes and take up less space when dried in a base sturdy enough to support them.

Silica gels and specially treated dry sands for drying flowers are available at your local craft store. Using these products will better preserve the color and shape of the flowers. These methods are only useful when preserving a few flowers, not large bunches.

Seeds are easiest to dry when you cut the stem with the flowerhead attached and store the entire cluster in a paper bag upside down until dry, shaking them loose later on. The paper bag method mentioned earlier is similar to this, and is best used on flowerheads that disperse their seeds too quickly. Once the seeds are dry, they should be stored in airtight containers and labelled.

Drying roots requires higher temperatures than flowers and leaves, around 120–140°F. Clean the roots, cut them into pieces and spread them out evenly on baking trays. Place the trays into a cool oven, with the door slightly open, then gradually turn the oven on to the lowest temperature setting to ensure even heat. Once the roots are brittle to the touch, take them out. Test the roots for doneness frequently—you don't want them to become browned or shriveled. The time it takes to dry the roots varies based on your oven, region and the moisture content and size of the root pieces.

free standing or attached to the wall, are made for just this purpose and allow enough surface area to dry herbs.

Leave herbs until crackly dry to the touch. The length of time will differ from one herb to another, based on a variety of factors. Once dried, separate the bundles and gently strip the leaves from the stems. Larger leaves that have already been separated from the stems can be crumbled into pieces for storing.

Dried flowers can either be left in bundles for later use, if kept in an area where nothing can damage them, or they can be cut from their stems and stored.

Large flowerheads such as roses should be cut from their stems. The petals can be separated and loosely spread out onto paper or trays to dry. Some flowers can be dried whole, such as calendula. The petals can be separated later for use, once dried. Other flowers, such as lavender, are best dried in bunches, loosely tied with string. The flowerheads can be covered with paper bags while drying to catch petals

Storing Dried Herbs

Airtight containers are the best method of storing dried herbs. Glass and wooden containers, airtight tins and paper bags are preferable to plastic ones. Plastic tends to encourage mold if there is a small amount of moisture left in the herbs. Dark and cool areas are the best places to store your herbs to preserve their oils, colors and flavors.

Frozen herbs can be used in any dishes that call for fresh or dried herbs.

For short-term storage, place leafy stems in between two layers of foil and refrigerate or place in a freezer bag and they will last 6–8 weeks.

For long-term storage, rinse freshly cut herbs in cold water and shake off any excess water. Remove the leaves from the tougher, older stems (unless it's a herb that has a useful stem), but leave tender young stems attached. Finely chop the herbs and pack into ice-cube trays. Top up with water and put in the freezer. Once frozen, put the frozen herb cubes into freezer bags for later use. Don't forget to label the bags, because the herbs can last 6–12 months when stored this way, and you're bound to forget what they are. The herb cubes can be used directly from the freezer to season soups, stews, casseroles and other dishes.

Herb-infused Oils and Vinegars

Preserving the flavors of herbs in vinegars and vegetable and olive oils is easy, and you can use these herbs in cooking, cosmetics and crafts. Herbal oils and vinegars can preserve a single flavor, such as basil, or a mixture of flavors, such as basil, oregano and thyme. Use three herbs or less per bottle; otherwise, the oil may become cloudy. Dishes including pasta, vegetables and meat will all benefit from the flavors

Safflowers in oil

Some people dip the leaves of their herbs in oil before placing them between layers of foil before freezing. Oil isn't necessary and can cause the leaves to become soggy once thawed.

and herbal perfumes preserved in oil or vinegar. Handmade herbal soaps and bath products are ideal for the fragrant oils in herbs such as rosemary.

It's important always to use a good quality, mild-flavored oil such as sunflower or safflower oil. The goal is to preserve the taste of the herb and not the oil. Olive oil is only suitable for strongly flavored herbs or when a subtle herb flavor is desired. Cover the herbs completely by the oil during the infusing process, and remove all plant material from the container before storing it long-term.

Tarragon vinegar

Cold-infused Oils

Cold-infused oils should be prepared in a clean, sterilized container, preferably glass. Add a handful of herbs to the container, crushing them slightly as they enter the container to release their essential oils. Pour the oil into the container until the herbs are completely covered. Cover the container and stand it in a warm location such as a sunny windowsill. Shake the container daily. After a week or so, strain the herbs from the oil and replace with another batch of the same herb or herbs. Leave for another week to further infuse the flavors. This process can be repeated until the flavor is to your liking, then remove the herbs from the oil and pour the oil into a clean, sterilized container with an airtight lid. The oil will keep for a several months. Keep the oil in a dark, cool location to ensure its longevity.

Make small batches of infused oil until you to know how often you use it. You don't want stagnant or rancid oil that you weren't able to finish using, and smaller batches will always leave you with freshly flavored oil.

Heat-infused Oils

Heat-infused oils are prepared by placing a ceramic or glass bowl over a pot of simmering water, just as you would melt chocolate. Pour the desired amount of oil into the bowl, and stir in your choice of fresh herbs. Let the mixture stand over low heat for up to three hours. Once cooled, strain out the bits and pour the oil into a dark-colored, sterilized bottle, seal tightly and store in a cool, dark place.

Infused vinegars can be prepared in the same way as oils. Infused herbal vinegars can be made with fresh, dried or frozen herbs. Flower petals, seeds, bulbs leaves and fruit can be added to vinegar just as they can be added into light oils. Savory herbal vinegars, such as tarragon vinegar, are fantastic when used on salads, while fruity vinegars add sharpness and a hint of sweetness to vegetable dishes. Fruit vinegars, such as one infused with raspberry, also work well to relieve a sore throat, and a compress wet with lavender vinegar can relieve a headache when applied to the forehead. Herbal vinegars often have antiseptic qualities.

Some homemade cosmetics call for a base of cider vinegar, which is said to restore the acid mantle of the skin. It is traditionally used in homemade hair rinses and skin lotions. Vinegars made with rose petals or a mixture of mint and marigold are great when diluted in water and used as facial toners. Because vinegar does not spoil as quickly as oil, you can make herbal vinegars in larger batches.

Preserving Herbs in Sugar

Sugar is an excellent medium for herbs and is useful in a variety of dishes, particularly desserts. Edible flowers can be crystallized in sugar by simply painting the petals with a thin coat of lightly whipped egg whites and covering them in caster or super fine sugar. The crystallized flowers are then spread out on a baking tray and placed into an oven on the lowest setting, only until completely dry and brittle, but not brown. They'll keep in airtight containers in the fridge or freezer for weeks if not months.

Sugar infused with the flavors of herbs such as lavender is a sweet addition to cakes, biscuits and cookies. It's worth having a small container of it on hand if you bake often. To create lavender sugar, simply add lavender flower spikes to some sugar, sieve the flowers from the sugar once the flavor is to your liking and store in an airtight container.

Herbal Honey

Herbs can also be preserved in honey. Choose the finest honey you can find and add your favorite herbs to a small quantity of honey in an airtight container. Once infused, the honey can be drizzled into herbal teas for a unique flavor or taken in teaspoonfuls to alleviate sore throats and cold symptoms.

Herbed Butter

Herbed butter is a tasty way to add flavor to many dishes. Savory breads and herbed butters are ideal matches, as are sandwiches, biscuits and scones. Herbed butter can be melted over a steaming cob of corn or just about any cooked vegetable. You can create all kinds of herb mixtures for butter, just as you would for herbal oils and vinegars; it just depends on your taste.

Dried and fresh sage, and sage butter

You'll have to experiment with the ratio of herbs to butter, but the general recommendation is 2–3 tbsp of finely chopped, fresh herbs for every 1lb of softened butter. You can also add edible flowers for color and flavor, and lemon juice and pepper to taste if you like. Once mixed, roll the butter into a log and wrap it in a layer or two of wax paper. Refrigerate until firm enough to slice into pats. Alternatively, pipe the butter into "kisses" onto a baking sheet and refrigerate for a couple of hours or until firm. The butter pats or kisses can be stored in airtight bags or containers in the refrigerator for up to three months. The combinations are limited only by your imagination.

What to Do with Your Herbs

Now that they're preserved, what creations can you whip up with your herbs? The culinary options are endless. There are few recipes that don't call for at least one herb, and even when they call for a particular herb, you may find that you prefer another or a combination of two or three to enhance the flavors of the dish.

Textile artists, dyers, spinners and crafters have been using herbs as natural dyes for centuries and for good reason. Natural dyes are non-toxic, easy to use, offer a range of beautiful colors and can be grown in your own backyard. Safflower flower petals offer warm yellow hues, as do tansy and other herbs with brightly colored flowers and foliage.

Use dyes and herbs in handmade toiletries such as soaps, lotions, hair rinses, cosmetics. Dyes lend warm color while herbs enhance fragrance, color and aromatherapeutic and homeopathic properties. Herbs can also improve the texture and color of handmade products such as candles, soaps and paper.

Once you've decided what to do with your treasured herbs, you'll find yourself experimenting more and more, trying to perfect your crafts, dishes and the environment around you. When we connect with the natural world, surrounding ourselves with plants and all the things they can be used to create, we find ourselves living more healthily and with a closer connection to nature, something that has been lost over the generations.

Have fun growing and nurturing your herbs. Enjoy everything they have to offer and treat all of your successes and failures as a part of a learning experience, because there is no right and wrong, only something to build upon.

The Language of Herbs

Herbs, particularly in the Victorian era, were used to represent different emotions and to symbolically communicate the heart's desires. Many of the meanings remain the same today, but without the scandalous intrigue.

Basil, for example, represents fidelity or love, whereas lavender means distrust. Lemon balm in an arrangement represents sympathy, and yarrow says "healing of the heart." Marjoram represents happiness, borage says courage and rosemary symbolizes remembrance.

Recipes and Craft Suggestions

Rose and Lemon Potpourri
3 tbsp orrisroot, premixed with 15 drops of rose oil

2 cups dried rosebuds and rose petals

1 cup dried rose-scented geranium leaves

1 cup dried lemon verbena

Combine the orrisroot and rose oil in a glass jar, screw the lid on tightly and shake well. Mix the remaining ingredients together and pour into the jar. Shake well again. Transfer into an airtight container and leave to infuse for at least two weeks. Remove what it is needed into a decorative dish or bowl and keep the remaining mixture in the airtight container for later use.

Dream Pillows
Dream pillows or sweet pillows are sachets or packets of herbs tucked between the pillow and pillowcase. The aroma released from the herbs supposedly improves sleep and may even help shape your dreams. Chamomile flowers are said, for example, to dispel nightmares and calendula flowers to promote auspicious dreams. Combining rose petals, lavender flowers and leaves and lemon verbena leaves produces a calming and soothing scent used in aromatherapy to assist in deep, restful sleep and stress reduction. To induce deep sleep, combine hops and chamomile flowers, peppermint and lavender leaves. The herbal packet or sachet can also be placed between the fitted sheet and mattress or hung from the headboard to prevent waking light sleepers.

Sachets

Sachets used purely for their fragrance are easy to make and can be used to scent just about anything, such as closets, trunks, rooms, suitcases or cars. What you choose to include in your sachet is up to you. A small pocket of linen or cotton, approximately the size of your palm, is ideal for stuffing with your favorite scented herbs. Finish it off with a strip of ribbon to put it wherever you desire a hit of fragrance.

Wreaths

Herbal wreaths, tussie mussies and herbal ropes are useful wherever you would like to add a little fragrance, but rather than hiding them away, these treasures can be. Lavender wreaths are lovely and add a delicate touch to a bedroom or. The steam from a bath or shower will help to bring out the essential oils of the leaves and flowers. Catnip is also another ideal herb for this purpose. Its flexible stems can be braided together, either alone or combined with other herbs, and used to scent vanities, wardrobes—even your cubicle at the office. Many herbs also possess natural insecticidal properties and help ward off moths and other critters that may harm your clothes.

Therapeutic, natural preparations for toiletries, bath products and cosmetics have made a huge comeback because of the known adverse affects of synthetic ingredients and chemical preservatives. What you apply to your body is as important as what you put into your body. The following are a few simply made products that you can integrate into your daily routine, and use to replace products harmful to you and the environment.

Rosewater Toner

⅔ cup rosewater

⅔ cup witch hazel

6 drops glycerin

Combine all of the ingredients into a container with a lid and shake before use. Use as a facial skin toner after washing, to refresh and invigorate the skin before moisturizing, particularly before bed.

Lip Balm

Combine two to three drops or more of lemon verbena, thyme, lavender, scented geranium, jasmine and peppermint or other essential oils you prefer, to 1 tbsp of warmed cocoa butter. Mix and transfer into a small jar, allowing it to cool. Once cool, apply a thin layer to the lips when dry.

Foot Bath

Sprinkle handfuls of individual portions of fresh bay leaves, lavender, thyme, lemon balm, marjoram and spearmint, or combinations thereof into a large bowl, with 2 tsp of salt and enough hot water to cover the feet and ankles. Submerge your tired feet into the hot water for at least 10 minutes for a soothing treat.

Lavender Spritz

Place a couple of drops of lavender oil into a small atomizer or spray bottle, with enough distilled water to fill the container. Shake to blend and spritz onto your face for an invigorating skin freshener.

Invigorating Herbal Bath

Add 2 tbsp each of sage, strawberry leaf and mint to a hot bath and soak for 20 minutes, drawing in the sweet aroma as the essential oils are released from the herbs onto your skin. Another ideal combination for a rejuventating and calming bath is 2 tbsp each of calendula petals, lavender, sweet marjoram, mint or rosemary.

Stimulating Marigold Bath

Add 1 cup of dried marigold petals and 1 tsp of baby oil into a warm, not hot, bath. Soak for at least 15 minutes. This combination is said to possess dehydrating properties and act as an astringent. This also works well with calendula petals.

Chamomile facial bath in sink (above), sorrel leaves can be steeped to create a facial bath (below)

Wild Garden Shower Soap

½ cup distilled water

½ cup orange flower water

1 tbsp dried peppermint leaves

1 tbsp dried chamomile

1 tbsp dried rose petals

1 tbsp orange blossoms

½ tbsp unscented glycerin soap

1 tsp castor oil

Combine the distilled water and orange flower water in a saucepan and bring to a boil. Remove the pan from the heat and add the dried peppermint, chamomile, rose petals and orange blossoms. Let steep for 1 hour. Strain the herbs and flowers from the water and reheat gently. Add the glycerin soap and stir in the castor oil. Let cool to room temperature and bottle. This shower soap is mild enough for everyday use.

Herbal Oatmeal Soap

This soothing soap is a great way to reconnect with nature through skin-loving herbs and oatmeal. It's great for dry skin and is easy to make with melt-and-pour soap you can purchase at any craft store. It yields approximately 17, 4 oz bars, depending on the size of the molds, and takes about 1–2 hours to make, including cooling time.

1 lb melt-and-pour soap base

¼ tsp rosemary essential oil

¼ tsp sage essential oil

¼ tsp lavender essential oil

1 cup oatmeal

¼ cup dried chamomile flowers

¼ cup calendula petals

⅛ cup dried rosemary

⅛ cup dried rose hips

1½ cups distilled water

Combine the water, oatmeal and herbs in a saucepan. Heat to boiling, then cover and let simmer a minimum of 30 minutes. Let cool, covered. When the mixture is cool enough to handle, strain it through a double- or triple-folded cheesecloth. Set aside. The resulting thick liquid is a slurry. Using a sharp knife, cut your melt-and-pour soap base into 1 inch cubes and place in a microwave-safe measuring bowl. Microwave on high for 30 seconds at a time, stirring periodically until the base is nearly melted. Remove and stir until all soap base pieces have melted. If you don't have a microwave oven, melt the soap in a double-boiler. Stir the base slowly and minimally to prevent any air bubbles. Handle the hot liquid with great care and let it cool down before you add the essential oils or the scents will vaporize. Add the herbal slurry and essential oils as soon as you can comfortably touch the mixture. Stir gently and pour into molds. Allow the soap to stand until it hardens. Place the molds into the freezer for 10 or 15 minutes or until the mixture is firm. Once the soap has hardened, it is easier to get out of the molds. The bars can be used immediately and will last for 6–12 months.

Basic Savory Herbal Infused Oil

4 tbsp fresh, chopped herbs, either all of one kind or a combination

2 cups of light oil, such as olive, sunflower or safflower

Crush the herbs and transfer into a bowl. Add the oil slowly. Coat the herbs with the oil and pour into a container with an airtight lid. Keep at room temperature for at least 2 weeks while the oils from the herbs infuse into the oil. Strain the herbs out of the oil and transfer the flavored oil into a jar or bottle.

Basic Herbal Infused Vinegar

2 cups white wine vinegar

4 sprigs of culinary herbs, sized to fit bottle, or 2 tbsp herb seeds such as fennel, coriander or dill

Pour the vinegar into a decorative, airtight bottle, until it reaches about 3" from the top. Add the herbal sprigs or seeds to the vinegar and seal with a lid or cap. Leave the bottle to infuse at room temperature for 2 weeks. Once infused, strain out the herbs or seeds and replace with fresh ones for a more intense flavor. Store the infused vinegar in the refrigerator.

Fragrant Thai Oil

2 stalks lemongrass, halved lengthwise

6 kaffir lime leaves or lime zest

2 slices fresh ginger

1 tiny red chili pepper

2 ½ cups sunflower oil

Lightly crush the ingredients and transfer into a wide-necked bottle. Fill with the sunflower oil and leave to infuse for up to 2 weeks. Store in a cool place when not in use. This spicy oil is ideal for drizzling over steamed fish or to enhance marinades. It also makes a tasty dip for salad rolls when mixed with rice vinegar.

Fennel and Lemon Butter
1 stick lightly salted, softened butter
2 tbsp chopped fennel leaves
grated zest of half a lemon
freshly ground pepper to taste

Combine the butter, fennel, lemon zest and pepper in a bowl and beat until evenly mixed. Smooth mixture onto plastic wrap and roll into a 1–2" wide log and chill until firm. Once firm, cut into pats and serve with fish or cooked vegetables. It is also quite tasty when sprinkled over popcorn.

Bouquet Garni and Fines Herbes
A *bouquet garni* is a bundle of herbs added to dishes such as stews and soups. Often this bundle includes parsley, marjoram, thyme and bay leaf. Basil, chervil, tarragon and salad burnet can be used, depending on the flavors desired. Herbs in a *bouquet garni* are tied together at the stem, enclosed in a cheesecloth bag and left to steep in the pot until the food is cooked. Remove the bag before serving the dish.

Fines herbes differ in that the herbs are finely chopped and sprinkled over the dish prior to cooking, and they are not removed before serving. Parsley is often the main herb used in French cooking. To Italian chefs, *fines herbes* refers specifically to flat-leaf rather than curly-leaf parsley. To many North American cooks, *fines herbes* is a

combination of chopped parsley, tarragon, chives and chervil. Other possibilities include rosemary, sage, marjoram, basil and oregano.

Poor Man's Capers (Pickled Nasturtium Seedpods)
green nasturtium seedpods
2 cups water
1 tbsp salt
garlic cloves, peeled
pickling spices
white wine vinegar, enough to fill jars
pickling jars, size of your choice

Soak green seedpods for 24 hours in a brine made from the water and salt. Drain. Pack small, sterilized jars with the drained seedpods. Include 1 peeled clove of garlic and 1 tsp of pickling spices in each jar. Heat white wine vinegar to simmering and fill each jar with the vinegar. Seal with acid-proof lids and let the seedpods sit for about a month. Eat pickled seedpods within a week of opening.

About this Guide

The plants featured here are organized alphabetically by their most common familiar names. Additional common names appear in the Features section of each entry. This system enables you to find a plant easily if you are familiar with only the common name. The scientific or botanical name is always listed after the common name. We encourage you to learn these botanical names. Several plants may share the same common name, and they vary from region to region. Only the specific botanical name identifies the specific plant anywhere in the world.

Clearly indicated within each entry are the plant's height and spread ranges, outstanding features and hardiness zone(s), if applicable. Each entry gives clear instructions for planting and growing the plants, and recommends many of our favourite selections. If height and spread ranges or hardiness zones are not given for every recommended plant, assume these ranges are the same as those provided in the Features section. Your local garden centre will have any additional information about the plant and will help you make your plant selections.

Finally, the Pests and Diseases section of the introduction deals with issues that afflict your garden plants from time to time. At the back of the book you will find a glossary and an index. The glossary provides definitions of some selected terms while the index can help you find specific plants by either their common or their botanical names.

Anise

Pimpinella

Anise has a wide variety of culinary uses, including in salads, desserts, candy and baked delicacies. Throughout history, the licorice scent of anise has been used in fragrances, liqueurs, cosmetics and even pharmaceutical products. This versatile herb may have fallen out of favor in our modern kitchens, but it is deserving of a place on your windowsill or in your garden, pantry, medicine cabinet and vanity.

Features
Other names: aniseed
Parts used: leaves, seeds and oil
Hardiness: half-hardy annual

Growing
Anise prefers to grow in **well-drained, rich** or **fertile, moist** and **sandy** soil. **Neutral to slightly alkaline** soil is best. Anise is best grown in a container throughout Washington and Oregon because of the acidic soil that is often found here. **Partial shade to full sun** will deliver the best results. A location sheltered from the wind will prevent the seeds from broadcasting themselves everywhere, leaving you little to harvest.

Grow anise from seed indoors in early spring or directly into the soil in late spring, depending on your zone's last frost dates.

Companion plant anise with coriander/cilantro because anise seeds will germinate more quickly if sown near coriander seed. Sow the seeds thickly so that the plants will help to support each other.

Tips
Because of its taproot, don't transplant anise. It grows well in a container or in the garden, as long as it is not moved. You'll likely need several anise plants to harvest a useful crop of seed.

Recommended
P. anisum is a half-hardy annual that grows roughly 18"–24" tall and 12" wide. The fragrant leaves are larger and more prominent toward the base of the plant, but more feathery, delicate and flattish toward the tips of the stems. White flowerheads bloom in mid- to late summer and are produced in an umbel form similar to dill. Aromatic, small

Anise flowers

brown seeds or fruit form once the flowers are spent.

Harvesting and Processing
Once the flowers are full of mature, brown seeds, cut the flowerheads off and place them in cardboard boxes, paper bags or on sheets of paper in a sunny location to dry. Rub the dried flowers between the palms of your hands to dislodge the seeds, and store the seeds in an airtight container.

Uses
Anise is most commonly used to make tea, but whole or ground seeds also taste wonderful in quick breads. Anise complements other flavors, and the seeds help aid digestion. This herb is frequently used in Indian and Moroccan cuisine and in cookies and other desserts.

Anise oil can be used topically as a fragrant antiseptic or in scented soaps, massage oils and handmade lotions.

Because anise seeds contain anethole, a plant hormone similar to human estrogen, women who are pregnant or nursing should avoid them.

Arugula

Eruca

Some consider this plant to be a vegetable while others think it's a herb, and they're both right. This peppery flavored plant is native to parts of Asia and southern Europe, while only naturalized in parts of North America. It is a relatively well-known plant that has experienced waves of popularity over the years. After close to two centuries of being overlooked, arugula is experiencing a new life in the Midwest. In fact, it's become quite fashionable, trendy even. It is deserving of such accolades, but I'd like to see it used in everyday cooking, rather than only in fancy bistros and restaurants, because it has so much to offer.

Arugula combines well with other herbs, including parsley, lovage, cilantro, basil, cresses, dill, borage and salad burnet.

Arugula salad and seeds

Features

Other names: salad rocket, roquette, rucola

Parts used: leaves, flowers, seeds

Hardiness: annual

Growing

Arugula prefers to grow in **full to partial sun. Cool, moist** and **rich** soil will help to produce more tender and less pungent leaves than dry, hot soil. Wait to sow seed until the risk of frost has passed. In the Midwest, it's a benefit to plant arugula seeds at the beginning of May so that harvest can start before the hot summer weather begins.

Tips

Arugula is best grown either in a vegetable or herb garden setting. Arugula doesn't lend itself well to container growing and is best grown in the ground outdoors. However, it is possible to grow arugula in pots. Make sure to sow the seed early in spring and use a bark/compost potting mix. Pinch the new leaves out frequently for use and maintain a good level of moisture without keeping the soil too wet. Be careful not to fertilize excessively because this results in lush leaves that lack flavor.

Recommended

E. vesicaria subsp. *sativa* is an upright annual with toothed leaves on tall stems tipped with four-petalled flowers in white, veined with purple, reminiscent of scented geranium flowers. Slender, erect seed pods follow after the flowers. It grows 24–36" tall but only 6–8" wide.

Arugula grows best in full sun.

Harvesting and Processing

The tender leaves are best when picked before the flower stems emerge because they become more pungent and somewhat bitter over time. The leaves are ready for harvest 6 to 8 weeks after sowing. They should always be used fresh, because drying them diminishes their flavor. Arugula does not freeze well.

Uses

Popular in Mediterranean cuisine, the peppery leaves of arugula are mainly used as a salad herb and are commonly found in mesclun, a mixture of salad greens originating in southern France, around Nice. When used in salads, arugula combines well with nutty oil dressings. The leaves can also be added to stir-fries, pasta sauces, potato salads or almost any dish where spinach is used. Arugula is particularly tasty in egg dishes; poached eggs on a bed of arugula leaves are delicious. It also blends beautifully with prosciutto, with mushrooms and with mild cheeses in sandwiches and hors d'oeuvres. Herbal butters, dressings and pesto,

Arugula in bloom (above and top left)

with or without basil, also benefit from arugula's lightly piquant flavor.

The flowers, seeds and an oil extract are also edible. The flowers, which taste citrusy, can be used as an edible garnish.

You may come across a plant called wild arugula, which is completely different from the one recommended here. Wild arugula, *Diplotaxis muralis*, is a perennial that produces leaves that are more ornate than, but just as pungent as, those of *Eruca vesicaria*. Turkish arugula, *Bunias orientalis*, produces leaves that resemble those of a dandelion.

Leaves taste more peppery as they age, but leaf flavor diminishes almost entirely once the flowers appear.

The leaves are aromatic, producing a peppery scent as they are harvested.

Harvested arugula leaves

Basil

Ocimum

Of any herb, basil is probably the one that has been grown by every level of green thumb. There is an amazing array to choose from in the basil family, and new introductions are revealed almost annually. The fragrant leaves of fresh basil add a delicious flavor to a wide variety of savory and sweet dishes, so it's no surprise that it is one of the mainstays of cooking today.

Basil flowers and leaves

Features

Parts used: leaves, seeds and oil
Hardiness: annual

Growing

Basil grows best in a **warm, sheltered** location in **full sun**. The soil should be **fertile, moist** and **well drained**. Pinch tips regularly to encourage bushy growth. Remove all flower spikes and fertilize with an organic fertilizer, such as compost tea, and you'll soon see a fresh crop of growth emerge.

Starting basil from seed can be a bit of a challenge, but if you're determined to give it a try, start the seed indoors 6 to 8 weeks before your frost date in order to plant the seedlings out in the spring after any risk of frost has passed.

Tips

Though basil will grow best in a warm spot outdoors in the garden, it can be grown successfully in a pot by a bright window indoors to provide you with fresh leaves all year.

Recommended

O. basilicum is a very frost-sensitive annual. Although there are many species, hybrids and cultivars to choose from, the tender leaves are easily damaged by both frost and lengthy periods of intense, direct sun. It produces aromatic, lush green and sometimes purple-flushed foliage in a bushy form, 12–24" tall and 12–18" wide. Purple- or pink- tinged flowers are produced in spikes above the foliage. The following are only a small sample of what is available: **'African Blue'** a hybrid with a warm, sweet, camphor scent and deep green, purple-veined leaves; **'Ararat'** bearing purple-marked foliage with a strong hint of anise flavor; **'Cinnamon'** has a clean, spicy aroma with a hint of cinnamon, distinctly veined foliage and purple-stained stems; **'Compatto'** is a compact form of **'Genovese,'** and both are standard, large-leaf selections and very flavorful; **'Greek Column'** is a hybrid that

O. basilicum 'Red Rubin' (above); basil seeds (below)

grows to 24–30" tall with an upright habit, but it seldom flowers; **'Magical Michael,'** a 2002 AAS recipient, bears red-veined foliage and stems, with a fruity aroma and burgundy flowers; **Var. minimum** (bush basil, Greek basil) is a dwarf selection with tiny, pungent leaves and white flowers; **'Mini Purpurescens Wellsweep'** forms a mound of dark purple foliage edged in bright green; **'Pesto Perpetual'** is another columnar form with variegated leaves; **'Pistou'** grows to 8" tall in a bushy, dwarf form; **'Purple Ruffles'** is another AAS winner with large, heavily ruffled and fringed, dark purple foliage and pink flowers; **'Siam Queen'** the 1997 AAS winner, bears dark purple flowers atop dark green leaves, with a spicy licorice flavor; **'Special Select'** is one of the best basils for pesto, bearing bright green leaves; **'Spicy Globe'** is a uniform bush basil with larger leaves; **'Sweet Dani,'** yet another AAS winner, produces the strongest lemon flavor and scent available on the market.

Harvesting and Processing

Pinch out the newest tips throughout the growing season for cooking. As fall approaches, closely watch the weather forecasts and ensure that you have cut the leafy stalks down for drying indoors long before a fall frost. Bunches can be air dried and stored in airtight containers; however, mold could set in if the leaves take too long to dry. The leaves can be chopped finely and mixed with a little water and frozen into ice cubes for cooking.

O. basilicum 'Purpurescens' (above); O. basilicum 'Siam Queen' (below)

If you chose to take your pots of basil indoors to use through the colder months, make sure to pinch the newest growth back often, to promote a stalky, bushy plant. Place it in a location with as much natural light as possible or under an artificial growing light.

Basil is a good companion plant for tomatoes—both like warm, moist growing conditions and when you pick tomatoes for a salad, you'll also remember to include a few leaves of basil.

Uses

Basil is used mostly for culinary purposes including soups, breads, casseroles, dips, spreads and so on. It's also very prevalent in certain cuisines, including Thai and Mediterranean. Cosmetic and medical uses are possible, but limited.

Not all types of basil are suitable for cooking; some are too strong or bitter, overwhelming a dish rather than complementing it.

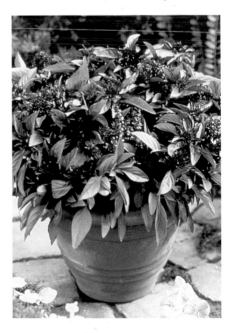

Bay
Laurus

Bay is positively one of the easiest herbs to grow. Its refined appearance and form are ideally suited to formal settings when trained and used as topiary in decorative containers. It's an undemanding plant that is happily transferred from a sunny window indoors to a lightly shaded spot outdoors when the weather allows.

Harvest bay leaves at any point. Some find the newest growth to be the tastiest while others find the "mid-age" leaves to be even tastier. You be the judge!

Features
Other names: bay laurel, sweet bay, Grecian bay
Parts used: leaves
Hardiness: zones 8–10; grown as a container plant

Growing
Bay grows well in **light shade, partial shade** or **full sun** in a sheltered location. The potting mix should be **moist** and **well drained**. Fertilize monthly with half-strength fertilizer. Because bay is a woody plant, starting from seed isn't generally recommended. Start with young plants grown in containers, which are easy to move when you have to take them inside for the winter.

Tips
Bay is an attractive, small shrub, useful as a structural point in a mixed container and as a specimen. Pinch it back to maintain a compact form or train it as a standard. Combine it with other herbs in themed containers.

Recommended
L. nobilis is an aromatic, evergreen tree or shrub that grows 12–36" tall and 12–24" wide, but can reach 40' heights where it is hardy. In a container it stays much smaller and can be pruned to maintain a suitable size. **'Angustifolia'** (willowleaf bay) has narrow, wavy-edged, pale green foliage while **'Aurea'** has golden yellow foliage.

Don't confuse *L. nobilis*, the "true" bay, with *Umbellularia californica*, or California bay, considered by some to be a reasonable substitute for *L. nobilis*, but it is poisonous. Use it for crafts, but don't eat it.

Naturally dried and freeze-dried bay leaves

Harvesting and Processing
Bay is familiar to most of us as the large, flat leaves we pick out of our stews or soups before serving. To dry the leaves, pick them from the stems and spread them out on a wire rack, or hang intact branches in a dry, airy place.

Uses
Cooks of many cuisines find bay leaves indispensable. Individual leaves are an essential ingredient in a "bouquet garni," a bundle that includes parsley, marjoram, thyme and a few peppercorns used to flavor soups and stews, and which is removed after cooking.

Add bay leaves to a facial steam bath containing a combination of other herbs, depending on your skin type. Chamomile flowers, rosemary, rose petals and bay leaves are perfect for normal skin types. Add dried bay leaves to potpourri blends and sleep pillows for insomnia.

Crafters use bay stems for wreaths and swags.

Beebalm

Monarda

Bergamot has a bit of a bad reputation for developing powdery mildew, but planting newer, mildew-resistant varieties and ensuring ample air circulation around the plant will help prevent this problem. The recommended section lists the most mildew-resistant varieties currently available. Among bergamot's assets are its abundant flowers, which attract all kinds of nectar-loving bugs and birds, and its lemon-scented leaves, which can be used to brew tea.

A refreshing bergamot facial steam bath

Features

Other names: Oswego tea, bergamot, horsemint
Parts used: leaves, flowers
Hardiness: zones 3–8

Growing

Bergamot grows well in **full sun**, **partial shade** or **full shade**. The soil should be of **average fertility**, **humus rich**, **moist** and **well drained**. Divide every two or three years in spring as new growth emerges.

To help prevent powdery mildew, thin stems in spring to increase air circulation. Plant in full sun; partial to heavy shade increases the possibility that mildew will form. If mildew strikes after flowering, cut the infected portions out, back to the healthy growth or about 6", and new flowers and healthy foliage will re-emerge.

This plant is named after the Spanish botanist and physician Nicholas Monardes (1493–1588).

Tips

Use bergamot beside a stream or pond, or in a lightly shaded, well-watered border.

Bergamot will attract bees, butterflies and hummingbirds to your garden. Avoid using pesticides that can seriously harm or kill these creatures, especially if you plan to ingest this plant, or any plant, in your garden.

Recommended

M. didyma is a bushy, mounding plant that forms a thick clump of stems. It grows 2–4' tall and spreads 12–24". Red or pink flowers are borne in late summer. **'Gardenview Scarlet'** bears large scarlet flowers and is moderately resistant to powdery mildew. **'Jacob Cline'** has deep red flowers, grows 3–4' tall and is very resistant to powdery mildew. **'Marshall's Delight'** doesn't come true to type from seed and must be propagated by cuttings or divisions. It is very resistant to powdery mildew and bears pink flowers. **'Panorama'**

Bergamot tea (above); *M. didyma* (below)

is a group of hybrids with flowers in scarlet, pink or salmon. **'Petite Delight'** is the first in a series of dwarf varieties. It grows to 12–18" tall and bears purply pink flowers. **'Raspberry Wine'** bears red wine-colored flowers. **'Rosy Purple'** reaches 3–4' heights and has deep purple-red flowers; **'Violet Queen'** grows equally tall and bears deep purple flowers.

Harvest and Processing

The leaves and flowers should be harvested in late summer when the plant is in full bloom for drying. Spread the flowers and leaves out on a wire rack in a shady, airy location and store when dry in airtight containers. Fresh bergamot leaves and flowers can be minced and mixed with water for freezing in ice cube trays.

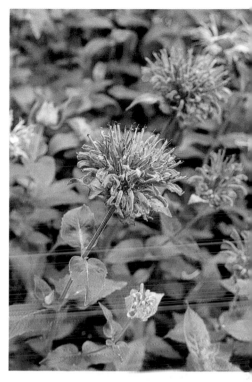

M. dıdyma (all photos this page)

Uses

The fresh or dried leaves may be used to make a refreshing, minty, citrus-scented tea. Put a handful of fresh leaves in a teapot, pour boiling water over the leaves and let steep for at least five minutes. Sweeten the tea with honey to taste. The leaves can be added to salads, cooling summer beverages, vegetable dishes, sweet jellies and even pork and veal dishes. Fresh or dried, the leaves can be used interchangeably with mint for a switch.

Cosmetically, bergamot can be used in a hot bath to perfume the water. Crafters frequently use the dried leaves in potpourri and their essence for bath oils, soaps and lotions.

As the name suggests, bergamot is extremely attractive to bees, hummingbirds and other pollinators. It's also a nectar source for butterflies.

Black Cumin

Nigella

This native of Asia was originally cultivated for its aromatic seeds and is still today, but it also has great ornamental appeal. Most gardeners are familiar with another species of Nigella, *N. damascena* or love-in-a-mist. The seed from this species is also used for culinary purposes, but *N. sativa* is the preferred species for cooking, particularly in Indian, Asian and Middle Eastern cuisine. The seeds impart a nutty or peppery flavor to food, with a hint of onion or caraway. Some even think the seeds taste like nutmeg or fennel. Similar to the subtleties of flavor displayed by a fine wine, black cumin reveals a variety of flavors and scents depending on the individual nose and palate. Black cumin is ideal to add to dishes with Mediterranean or Asian flavors. You'll find this one herb you can't cook without.

If you can find the essential oil processed from the seed of this herb, it has moth-repellant properties. Add a drop or two to sachets for wardrobes, chests and closets.

Black cumin seeds

Features
Other names: fennel flower, Russian caraway, black caraway, nutmeg flower, Roman coriander, black onion seed
Parts used: seeds, oil
Hardiness: annual

Growing
Black cumin prefers to grow in a location with **well-drained** soil and in **full sun**. This annual can be started by seed indoors. Simply transplant the seedlings into the garden or into containers after the last frost in spring. The seed can also be sown directly into the garden throughout the spring for summer blooming.

Tips
Similar to its relative, love-in-a-mist, black cumin is a pretty and interesting looking annual. It works well in containers when mixed with broad-leaved plants. It is also very attractive in mixed perennial and annual beds and borders. Borders around herb and vegetable gardens are also ideal for this annual, for a little added interest and a delicate touch.

Recommended
N. sativa is an erect, branching annual with finely dissected, grey-green leaves up to 2" long. This species produces small, white flowers with a blue tinge in summer. The flowers are followed by large, inflated fruits, or seed capsules, with spiky styles. Each fruit or seed capsule is divided into five compartments, each one topped with a spiky style resembling a horn or claw. It grows 12–18" tall and 9–12" wide.

Harvesting and Processing
Collect seeds in the fall, once ripe and after the seed capsule is dry. Gently open the seed capsule to release the seeds. Store seeds in an airtight container, in a cool and dry location.

Uses
Black cumin is delicious baked into flat breads, crackers, pastries and biscuits. It is commonly used in curries, dhals, Russian rye bread, and meat, fish and vegetable dishes. Its unique flavor complements chutneys, sauces and pickles. Its seeds are said to have medicinal properties, including numerous essential fatty acids, beneficial to the immune system, the skin, the lungs and the digestive tract.

Put the seeds in muslin bags to hang near the fireplace or other heat source, to fill the room with their delicious scent.

Borage

Borago

Borage is a vigorous, tenacious annual herb. It is valued by some but disliked by others because of its natural inclination to reseed itself everywhere. The flowers and foliage are not only pretty, but also delicious when used in salads, desserts, tea and sweet and cold beverages.

Use borage leaves in small amounts when cooking because they contain a compound that could be toxic if consumed in large quantities.

Features

Other names: cool-tankard, talewort, bee bread
Parts used: flowers, leaves (with caution)
Hardiness: zones 5–10

Growing

Borage prefers **full sun** but will also thrive in partial shade. **Moist, sandy, well-drained** soil is best. Borage is drought tolerant once established. Remove any unwanted seedlings as they emerge in early spring to prevent an onslaught of plants.

Tips

Plant borage in your vegetable or herb garden to attract bees for pollination. As an ornamental, it contrasts beautifully with dark foliage specimens. Borage will grow with wild abandon in dry, hot areas where little else will grow.

Recommended

B. officinalis is an upright plant with high clusters of pendent, violet-blue, star-shaped flowers in spring. The stems and foliage are covered in silvery hairs that complement the bluish flowers. It grows 24" tall and 12" wide.

Harvesting and Processing

Borage is best enjoyed throughout the growing season because the leaves and flowers are almost impossible to preserve or dry for later use. Pick young and immature leaves shortly before use. Mature leaves are better suited for use in herbal teas and cold summer soups.

Candy the flowers for desserts by removing the black anthers, lightly brushing the petals with gently whipped egg whites and dusting with super-fine sugar. Let dry.

Candied borage flowers

Adding flowers to your ice cube trays will preserve them for cold drinks beyond the growing season.

Borage has abundant medicinal properties. Borage is still considered to be an all-purpose herb and a must-have in the herbalist's kit. It's also beloved by beekeepers and gardeners for its attractiveness to pollinating insects.

Uses

The young leaves add a cucumber flavor to salads and sandwiches. The blossoms can be scattered over fruit cups and in cool, refreshing drinks, including iced tea and lemonade. The fresh flavor of the leaves is also a light and subtle complement to chicken and fish dishes.

Calamint

Calamintha

This fragrant, aromatic and tasty perennial deserves a bigger place in our gardens and pantries. Cooks may be familiar with lesser calamint (*C. nepeta*), or common calamint (*C. sylvatica*), which is a little less pungent but used in the same way. Related to savory, calamints are very versatile and useful in a number of dishes. The entire plant is reminiscent of mint with notes of thyme and camphor. It is warm and refreshing in the mouth, peppery with a light bitterness. It is easy to grow and is adorable in the landscape, producing softly colored fuzzy leaves and tubular flowers whose shape resembles pouting lips.

Features

Parts used: whole plant, leaves
Hardiness: zones 5–10

Growing

Calamint prefers to grow in a location with **full sun**. It can tolerate partial shade. The soil should be **alkaline, well-drained** and of **average fertility**. It can be propagated by division or grown from seed.

Tips

A herb garden is an ideal location for this plant because of its practical uses, but calamint is also a beautiful plant worthy of a place in the perennial border. It should be planted in groups for a bigger impact. Calamint can be grown in containers but only outdoors.

Dried calamint

Recommended

C. grandiflora (calamint, large-flowered calamint, showy savory) is a hardy perennial that produces square stems that arise from creeping rootstock. Flower spikes with lilac pink flowers swirl around the tall stems that rise up to 24" in height. Mint-scented, toothed, oval leaves are produced sparingly along those stems. This species spreads 12". 'Variegata' produces cream variegated leaves, but the seedlings are usually green.

C. nepeta (lesser calamint, nepitella, mountain balm) is a perennial that produces small, bicolored purple and white flowers on stems covered with pale grey, downy leaves.

C. sylvatica (common calamint) is a hardy plant with hairy, mint-scented, toothed leaves and pale lilac-colored flowers with darker spots. It grows up to 24" tall.

Harvesting and Processing

Harvest the leaves at any time, regardless of flowering. If drying the leaves, harvest and spread them out onto screens or hang them by their stems in bunches on drying racks. Once dried, store in airtight containers.

Uses

Sprinkle the young, minty leaves of lesser calamint into salads and tea for a refreshing boost. Calamint complements roasts, stews, game and fish, is wonderful with lentils, beans, eggplant and potatoes; and works well in sauces, marinades and stuffings. Lesser calamint is also a staple herb in Sicily, Sardinia and Tuscany where it is commonly used with vegetable and mushroom dishes. Calamint is used as a mild form of mint in Turkish cuisine. It also blends well with herbs such as bay, garlic, oregano, parsley, pepper, thyme, sage and mint. Fresh leaves are best for cooking while dried leaves are better for teas.

Calendula

Calendula

Calendula is the perfect annual. It is a relatively low-maintenance plant; it produces abundant seeds that can be shared with friends; its flowers look lovely cut for arrangements, and its seedlings sprout every year in places that need a bit of sunshine. This plant is so useful, I can't imagine a garden without it. For butterflies, it produces a seemingly endless supply of nectar. For people, the petals add a piquant note to green salads. Herbalists have made many claims for its curative powers, and few side effects have been recorded.

Calendula infused toiletries

Features

Other names: pot marigold, English marigold
Parts used: flowers
Hardiness: annual

Growing

Calendula does equally well in **full sun** or **partial shade**. It likes cool weather and can withstand a light frost. The soil should be of **average fertility** and **well drained**. A second sowing in mid-summer gives a good fall display. Deadhead to prolong blooming and keep plants looking neat.

Tips

These informal plants are attractive in borders and mixed into the vegetable patch. They can also be used in mixed planters. These cold-hardy annuals often continue flowering until the ground freezes completely.

Recommended

C. officinalis is a vigorous, tough, upright plant; it bears single or double daisy-like flowers in a wide range of yellow and orange shades. This plant grows 12–24" tall, with a slightly lesser spread. **'Bon Bon'** is a dwarf plant that grows 10–12" tall and comes in all colors. **'Fiesta Gitana'** ('Gypsy Festival') is a dwarf plant with flowers in a wide range of colors. **'Pacific Beauty'** is a larger plant, growing about 18" tall. It bears large flowers in varied colors.

Harvesting and Processing

The petals and whole flowers can be picked throughout the blooming cycle. They can be used fresh or dried, as well as in infused oil preparations which are made by steeping petals in warm vegetable oil. The oil will last for a few weeks at room temperature. The petals can also be frozen into ice

Calendula mixed with dill and poppies (above); nasturtiums and calendula (below)

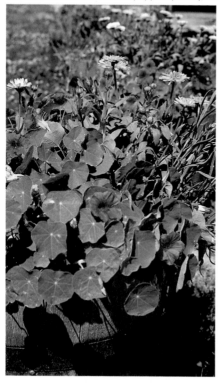

cubes for cool drinks or cooking once the blooming cycle is complete.

Uses

Also known as "poor man's saffron," calendula flowers are popular kitchen herbs that can be added to stews for color and flavor. The petals also add lively color to pasta, rice, potatoes, cakes and muffins. Eaten fresh, they have a slightly bitter flavor, but they mellow after cooking. Tossed into salads, fresh petals offer nutrition in the form of lutein, a powerful antioxidant. Combined with mint or lemon-flavored herbs, calendula petals are a pleasant addition to herbal teas.

Calendula flowers are appreciated equally for cosmetic, craft and cooking purposes. Anti-inflammatory, antiseptic, antibacterial and antifungal properties are all present in those

C. officinalis 'Apricot Sunrise' (above); calendula and bachelors buttons (below)

bright little petals. Because of these properties, the petals are often used in ointments for soothing irritated and chapped skin, eczema, insect bites and sunburns. They are also used in handmade creams and soaps for the face and hands.

Medicinally, calendula can be brewed into an infusion that can be used to wash minor cuts and bruises.

The name calendula comes form the Latin kalendae *which translates to "first day of the month," in the Roman calendar. Calendula tend to flower at the beginning of most months of the year.*

Caraway

Carum

Caraway is one of those herbs that isn't always considered when planting a herb garden, but it has many uses and deserves to become a Midwest landscape staple. Little is wasted because most of the plant can be used in a variety of tasty treats. Many cultures use caraway in foods such as cookies, breads, cakes, stewed fruit, cabbage and meat dishes as well as to flavor cheeses and to garnish salads. It also flavors a liqueur called Kümmel. The possibilities for caraway may not be endless, but having it in your garden or in a pot on your windowsill will open up new taste sensations in your everyday cooking.

Caraway seeds

Features
Parts used: leaves, seeds, root, essential oil from the seeds
Hardiness: zones 3–9, biennial

Growing
Caraway prefers to grow in **full sun**. The soil should be **deep, fertile** and **well drained**. Caraway will tolerate heavier soils. Because of its biennial nature, seed is borne in the second summer. Caraway does not transplant well because of its taproot. It's best to directly sow seed into the location where it will spend its life.

Caraway was once believed to keep lovers true to each other, hence its title as "the herb of fidelity."

Tips
Caraway is a finely detailed, delicate plant, bearing umbels of white flowers. Its graceful appearance complements bolder-leaved plants in mixed beds and borders. Caraway can also be grown in containers, but only in pots deep enough to accommodate the taproot over time. It is also ideal when planted in large groupings for impact in herb gardens.

Recommended
C. carvi is a 24" tall biennial that produces very feathery or fern-like foliage. Clusters of white flowers tower above the foliage and appear only in the plant's second year of growth. Ridged fruits or seeds follow after the flowers.

Harvesting and Processing
The feathery leaves can be used fresh in salads, stews and vegetable stir-fries. The seeds are the most commonly used part of the plant and should be harvested from the plant

before they fall to the ground. The seeds ripen roughly one month after the flowers are finished. Once the seeds turn brown, harvest by cutting the seedheads from the stems, carefully placing them into a brown paper bag, and allowing the seeds to freely fall when completely ripe. Keep the bag in a dry and warm location with adequate air circulation.

The roots can be dug after the second season, and once the harvest foliage and flowerheads have been removed. If you have room in your garden, sow a second crop of caraway strictly for the root because it's best when it's young and tender. It can be peeled and cooked liked a parsnip.

Uses
Many people have probably had a piece of rye bread with caraway seeds at one time or another, but that's certainly not the only use for caraway.

Flowering caraway (opposite & above); caraway seeds (below)

Dishes made with such vegetables as cauliflower, carrots and parsnips are the ideal base for caraway. Popular in German and Austrian cuisine, caraway seeds are thought to diminish the odor caused from cooking cabbage, not to mention add a subtle new flavor to this leafy side dish. Young leaves can be added to soups, salads and sandwiches for a mild dill-like flavor.

The flavor released from the seeds can change during cooking, so it's best to add the seeds during the last 10 to 15 minutes of cooking or baking.

Caraway seeds have been used medicinally to help settle an upset stomach. Crush and steep a tiny amount in boiling water or warm milk. Crush the seeds before steeping to release the beneficial compounds.

Catnip · Catmint

Nepeta

Cat lovers are more than familiar with the positive attributes of catnip and catmint, but gardeners may not be as familiar with the uses specific and help-ful to humans. In the garden, catnip has been found to be a natural insect repellent against aphids, Colorado potato beetles and squash bugs, perfect for the organic gardener. Also, the chemical *nepetalactone* found in the leaves of these herbs make both catnip and catmint unattractive to deer. Its uses don't end there, however, as catnip has so much more to offer beyond the entertainment value of watching your cats roll around on the floor.

Flowering catnip wreath

Features
Other names: dog mint, nep-in-a-hedge
Parts used: leaves, flowers and stems
Hardiness: zones 3–7

Growing
Both plants grow well in **full sun** or **partial shade**. Soil should be of **average fertility** and **well drained**. Plants will tend to flop over in rich soil. Pinch tips throughout the growing season to delay flowering and make the plants more compact. Once they are almost finished blooming, cut them back by one-third to one-half. This will encourage new growth and might prompt them to bloom again in late summer or fall. Divide in spring or fall when the growth begins to look overgrown and dense.

Tips
Use catnip and catmint to edge borders and pathways, or plant them with roses in a herb garden. Both are also great for containers, alone or mixed with other plants. In cool summer areas of the Midwest, catnip can be used as a substitute for heat-loving lavender as a pathway border with a purple haze.

Recommended
N. cataria is a short-lived, hardy perennial that produces aromatic, coarsely textured foliage with scalloped edges. This erect, bushy plant bears spike-like flowers in light shades of pink and purple all summer. It is also a prolific self-seeder. The species will grow approximately 36" tall and 12–18" wide. **'Citriodora'** is a lemon-scented cultivar that is

available but may be difficult to find. It is well worth the search, however.

N. x *faassenii* is a less intense version of catnip, better known as catmint, but is drought tolerant and longer lived in the garden. Its silvery leaves and violet blue flowers blend well in any garden. Habit can range from 10–30" tall and 10–36" wide, depending on the cultivar. '**Walker's Low**' is a vigorous plant that grows to 30" tall and 36" wide. It was also the Perennial Plant Association's 2007 Plant of the Year.

Harvesting and Processing
Pinching the tips or newest growth from the stems throughout the growing season is best. This will encourage the plant to branch out and remain dense. In regions with a fall killing frost, cut the stems to the ground just before hard frost and hang in bunches in a warm area with

Flowering catnip with celeriac, thyme, rosemary, peppers and dandelion (above left), dried catnip leaves and flowers (below left), catnip, greenleaf lettuce, Vietnamese coriander (below)

adequate air circulation. The dried leaves, flowers and stems can be used for months after they've thoroughly dried.

N. x *faassenii* 'Dropmore Blue' with goat's beard and daylily (above); flowering catnip in raised bed (below)

Uses

Catnip has long been cultivated for its reputed medicinal and culinary qualities. The leaves can be steeped in boiling water to make catnip tea, said to reduce nervous tension and anxiety, induce sleep and lower a fever. Regardless of the effect it may have, the magnesium and manganese it contains are sure to be a health benefit. Fresh leaves can be chopped up for soups, sauces, stews, pasta and vegetable dishes. The youngest tips can be minced and sprinkled on salads for extra flavor.

Crafters can use dried catnip in potpourri and arrangements in areas of the house where the aroma can be most enjoyed. Leafy catnip and catmint stems can also be intertwined with the stems of lemon balm, lemon verbena, marjoram, a variety of mints and scented geraniums into small wreaths or herbal garlands to hang in your closets and pantries.

Catnip is not prone to pests. However, the roots and crown can suffer from rot during cold and wet winters.

Chenopodium

Chenopodium

Good King Henry, fat hen, American wormseed, epazote, lamb's quarters, goosefoot, ambrosia and huizontle are names that may sound more familiar than the genus or botanical name for this herb, but there are too many great species to list just one. With each species comes a different list of uses, some of which are noted here. Mostly chenopodium is used in the kitchen and is definitely worth experimenting with because it offers a variety of health benefits and kick things up a notch in your cooking. Herbs from this unique and versatile genus are staples in the diets of some cultures, and are considered more vegetable than herb.

Features
Other names: goosefoot
Parts used: leaves, flower spikes
Hardiness: zones 3–9 and annual

Growing
All species of chenopodium prefer a location in **full sun**. The soil should be **well-drained, light** and **rich with organic matter**. Hardy species that have spent a year or more in a container should be divided and repotted annually in spring and amended with new compost.

Tips
Chenopodium species are attractive in the middle to back of borders and have more impact when mass planted. They can also be integrated into herb and vegetable gardens or grown in containers on the deck or balcony.

Recommended
C. album (fat hen, lamb's quarters, white goosefoot, common pigweed, all good, muckweed) is a tall growing annual that produces small, greenish-white flowers and arrowhead-shaped leaves.

C. bonus-henricus (good King Henry) produces small clusters of green-yellow flowers and triangular or arrowhead-shaped, deep green foliage with a coarse texture. The flowers are borne in tall flower spikes.

Harvesting and Processing
Chenopodium needs at least one year to develop before harvesting. Those in colder zones should plant the hardier species rather than the annual, to allow time for the plant to develop. After a year's growth, the young shoots can be harvested in mid-spring and eaten like asparagus. Harvest flowering spikes as they begin to open. Collect larger leaves later in the season and use as a spin-

Steamed chenopodium

ach substitute. Use leaves when fresh or fresh-frozen. Frozen leaves should be only used in cooked dishes. To freeze, use the ice cube method.

Uses
The leaves are rich in vitamin B1, C, calcium, iron and are helpful to those who suffer from anemia. Crushing the leaves results in a useful dye. The flower spikes can be steamed, tossed in butter and eaten like broccoli. The young leaves can be used raw in salads or in cooked dishes such as casseroles, stuffings, purées, soups and spicy pies. Leaves from any of the chenopodim species are more nutritious than cabbage or spinach leaves. The shoots can be blanched in hot water, followed by a quick dip in cold water to stop the cooking process, and used in a variety of dishes. The shoots can also be steamed or blanched. Peel only if necessary and serve with a variety of vinaigrette dressings.

The seed of *C. album* can be ground into a flour and used to make a thin version of oatmeal or hot cereal.

Chervil
Anthriscus

Chervil has earned its rightful place in the kitchen. It's been used for centuries for various culinary purposes and by homeopaths for medicinal purposes, but it's also grown by gardeners for its delicate beauty.

Features
Other names: French-parsley
Parts used: leaves
Hardiness: annual

Growing

Chervil grows well in **partial shade**, in any **well-drained, moist soil**. Sow seed directly into the soil, whether in the ground or in a container, because the seedlings are too delicate to transplant. This frost-tender herb should only be sown after the risk of frost has passed.

Chervil can go to seed very quickly in locations with hot summers. To prevent this from occurring, pinch the flowers out as they begin to emerge, allowing the plant to divert its energy into dense, leafy growth.

Tips

Chervil can be grown in a herbal garden for culinary or medicinal purposes, but it also works well in an ornamental setting. The delicate, divided leaves are the perfect foil for bold-leaved plants such as cannas, colocasia and hostas.

Recommended

A. cerefolium is an erect-growing annual with scented, deeply divided foliage that appears almost ferny in nature. The flavor and scent of the foliage is a cross between parsley and anise. The white flower clusters emerge on tall stems in summer. It grows 12" tall and 12" wide. *A. cerefolium* subsp. *crispum* (curly-leaved chervil) is similar to the species with a less palatable flavor.

Harvesting and Processing

The leaves can be harvested six to eight weeks after planting and throughout the season. The most flavorful leaves are the youngest, produced prior to flowering. Continue to pinch the flowers off before they open while harvesting the

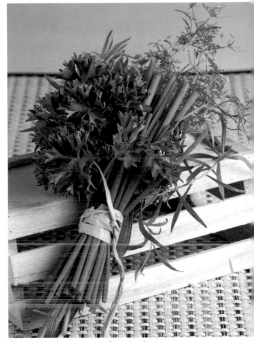

Chervil is often used in *fines herbes*.

leaves for use. The leaves can be dried as well, but they lose much of their flavor and effectiveness.

Uses

Chervil has been used traditionally as one of the four fragrant herbs that make up the delicate bouquet called *fines herbes* in French cuisine. This herb bundle combines chervil with chives, tarragon and parsley, in equal parts, and all finely chopped. Chervil has a delicate parsley-like flavor and is sometimes used in its place. Chervil's light flavor combines well with eggs, poultry and soft cheeses. Best used fresh, the leaves can be preserved frozen in ice cube trays for use all year long.

Medicinally, chervil can be steeped to make an infusion that stimulates digestion and relieves head colds.

Chicory

Cichorium

Chicory has been an important herb and vegetable for thousands of years. Its properties range from medicinal to culinary, and it was once relied upon as a "floral clock" because of the regular opening and closing of its flowers, opening to the sun and closing roughly five hours later. Roasted, ground chicory roots have been used to make a coffee-like drink since the 17th century. Charles Dickens went so far to recommend the warm beverage in his magazine, *Household Words*, more than 200 years after it was first used for that purpose. Once you discover the many ways you can used this herb, you'll find yourself adding it to your herb garden for something a little different.

Chicory leaves are often blanched by excluding light, either by removing all the leaves and then earthing up the new growth, or by covering the plant with a bucket or something similar.

Radicchio, also known as Italian chicory

Features

Other names: endive, succory, wild chicory, radicchio
Parts used: leaves, roots
Hardiness: zones 4–8

Growing

Chicory prefers to grow in **full sun**. The soil should be **well drained** and **fertile**. Seed can be sown directly or into containers in early spring. Seedlings can be planted out once the risk of frost has passed unless they're hardened off, in which case they can be planted sooner.

Tips

Chicory, like any herb, is always a fine addition to a herb garden, but the pretty violet blue flowers are attractive enough to mix into a flowerbed for an addition to the summer's profusion of blooms. It is a little too large for containers, however, unless you can provide some type of support like an obelisk.

Recommended

C. intybus is a clump-forming perennial that grows up to 4' tall and 24" wide. Toothed, tongue-shaped leaves are produced along with bluish purple, cornflower-like flowers. Occasionally, white or pink flowers are produced as well. This plant has a substantial taproot.

There are different types or phases of chicory, depending on what you're growing the plant for. The following types are grown for their leaves, which grow in both a head form similar to lettuce and on the stems above the basal leaves, prior to flowering.

Non-forcing chicory selections are available, including **'Crystal Head,'** **'Sugar Loaf'** (Pain de Sucre) and **'Snowflake.'** The leaves of non-forcing selections do not require blanching. Blanching refers to types which are grown without light, resulting in "bleached" leaves. **'Red Verona,'** **'Rosso di Chioggia'** and **'Rosso di Treviso'**

C. intybus (above); *C. intybus* in bloom (opposite page, below)

offer reddish colored leaves and are great additions to salads. **Witloof** (Brussels chicory) is grown for its chicons, or small, pastel yellow heads, and requires blanching to preserve its mild flavor.

'**Magdeburg**' or '**Brunswick**' are the best selections for producing roots that can be used as a coffee substitute.

Harvesting and Processing

The newest leaves, harvested from the stems, can be picked throughout the growing season. The older leaves tend to be quite bitter. The leaves can be eaten fresh but also dried. For drying, pick unblemished, young leaves and spread them out on a wire rack in a cool, dark place with adequate air circulation. Once dry, place the leaves into an airtight container.

Whole, washed leaves can be frozen in foil for weeks or chopped and mixed with a little water in ice cube trays.

Types that are grown for their heads, or chicons, should be harvested when very young, when they are tender and not bitter. To preserve the light leaf coloration, these selections should be grown without light, by either mounding soil over top or by placing an overturned bucket on top of the plant to shield it from light. Another method of blanching is to dig out the number of roots you require for heads in the fall. Remove the foliage and replant the roots tightly together and upright, in a deep box or pot with a sandy soil piled 6" above the tops of the roots. The roots should be kept in a moist, dark and heated location such as a greenhouse or warm shed (for large quantities) or in your house (for a pot or two). It's important for the area to remain very dark; otherwise, the leaves growing underneath the soil may begin to turn green and bitter. As soon as the white leaves begin to show above the soil, the plants are ready for lifting. Once lifted, the blanched, leafy head can be separated from the root.

The leaves used for tea are harvested from the taller stems or stalks that form if the plant is allowed to grow beyond the "lettuce" stage. The leaves can be used fresh or dried.

The roots can be harvested at any point. In order to use the roots as a coffee substitute, they have to be roasted. To roast chicory, chop fresh roots, place a single layer on a cookie sheet and roast in a 325°F oven for about 30 minutes, stirring every 10 minutes.

Ground chicory root

Uses

Either on its own or combined with other herbs, roasted chicory root makes a fine substitute for coffee. Simply combine 2 teaspoons dried, chopped burdock root, 1 teaspoon each roasted chicory root and dried, chopped dandelion root, 1/2 oz licorice root and 1 quart water. Combine herbs and water, simmer on low heat 20 to 30 minutes, strain herbs and serve. Sweetener and/or milk can be added to taste. As mentioned, the stem leaves can be used for medicinal purposes, such as in a tea for digestive upset, among other ailments.

When chicory has been grown for blanching, it's often used more as a vegetable than as a herb. Eat it raw in salads and sandwiches, boil the leaves and add them to cheese sauces, or serve them as a side vegetable.

Chili Pepper

Capsicum

Peppers are fruits that can also be considered vegetables or herbs. For our purposes, the smaller, hotter peppers will be our focus because they are used more often to flavor foods whereas, bell peppers are sometimes the main component of a meal. The list of uses for peppers grows every day, both culinary and medicinal. Certain cuisines—Mexican, Caribbean, African, Southeast Asian and Chinese—are synonymous with peppers and their spicy heat. Aside from heat, peppers can also add earthy, spicy and sweet notes to just about any dish.

Remove seeds from chili peppers to reduce their heat.

Features

Other names: cayenne pepper, hot pepper, chili pepper, paprika
Parts used: fruit
Hardiness: true annual or tender perennial, often grown as an annual or container plant

Growing

Peppers prefer **bright light in direct sunlight.** The soil should be **moist, well drained** and **fertile.** Mist the foliage often when growing indoors in regions with low humidity. Hot dry air is detrimental to peppers. Watch for signs of shrivelled and dropping foliage and fruit. Misting will also prevent the onset of a spider mite infestation. Pinch the tips of young plants to encourage branching. Wait to plant out seedlings until the risk of frost has passed and the soil has had time to warm. To ensure good pollination, grow at least two to three plants together, either in the same garden plot or in the same window. The hotter the weather, the hotter the pepper.

Tips

Peppers are considered short-term plants; however, they can be kept for up to two to three years indoors in the right conditions. Place them outdoors in the summer to ensure pollination when in flower. They can also be grown in a vegetable or herb garden during the summer months. The growing season is long enough to ensure time for pollination and fruiting.

The juice from the fruit is a powerful irritant, so thoroughly wash your hands before touching your nose or eyes after handling chili peppers.

Recommended

Capsicum annuum var. *annuum*, produces 4" long, oval leaves on thin stems in a bushy dense form. Small, inconspicuous, white flowers are followed by colorful, cone-shaped or rounded, upright fruit in shades of yellow, red and orange. Selections are available with speckled or mottled fruit as well. The following are only

C. chinense habenero peppers

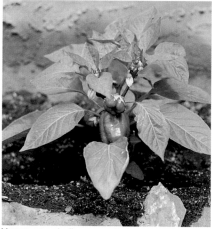

Young green bell pepper plant

Cayenne pepper plant in a mixed planter

a few of the selections available. There are five main groups of pepper cultivars: *Cerasiforme* (cherry), *Conioides* (cone), *Fasciculatum* (red cone), *Grossum* (pimento, sweet or bell pepper), and *Longum* (cayenne, chili).

'Anaheim' produces 6" long red peppers; 'Ancho' bears brick red to black-purple fruits, 4" long and 3" wide; 'De Arbol' is a cayenne type of pepper, 2–3" in length and hot; 'Jalapeno' is one of the most well known peppers, medium in heat and 2–3" in length; 'Jamaican Yellow' is very hot, green to bright yellow and mushroom shaped; 'Long Slim,' 'Mulato, and 'Pasilla' (poblano chile pepper) dry to a dark raisin brown, are 5–6" long and are of mild to medium intensity; 'Serrano' is 1" long and of medium hotness, and should be used when green or ripened to scarlet; 'Tabasco,' the pepper used to make the sauce, produces red fruits that point up to the sky and start out green, then turn yellow before ripening into a bright red; 'Thai' is another hot selection, bearing finger-sized fruit.

C. chinense habenero produces small 2" long fruits. They are the hottest of the hot, up to 50 times hotter than a Jalapeno pepper. When ripe, they resemble tiny bell peppers in bright yellow. 'Scotch Bonnet,' famous for being extremely hot, has an apple-cherry flavor.

Harvesting and Processing

Peppers can be harvested at varied stages of growth, depending on the variety and how hot you want them to be. Peppers can be used while they're still green, but wait until they've turned red if your intention

Dried peppers not only spice up your food, they supply vitamins and minerals.

is to dry the fruits for later use. Hot peppers or smaller peppers are great for drying because of their thin skin. Once harvested, the fruits can be threaded onto strings for hanging in a cool and airy location to dry. Once they're dry, they can be stored whole in a glass jar or airtight container. They can also be ground down into a powder or flakes.

Uses

Peppers are useful in many dishes, including stir-fries, appetizers, salads and sandwiches. Even the smallest peppers can be stuffed with savory mixtures of herbs and cheeses. Peppers can also be pickled and stuffed later on or eaten as-is as a snack.

Peppers are rich in vitamins A and C as well as mineral salts and have antibacterial properties. Pungent peppers are said to increase blood flow, stimulate the appetite, aid digestion and fight colds, fevers and sore throats.

C. 'Long Red' peppers

Capsicum *derives from the Greek* kapto, *to bite.*

Chives

Allium

Chives have been in people's gardens for over 5000 years, and today this herb knows no geographical limit. The delicate onion flavor of chives is the mildest in the onion family. Chives are also one of the easiest herbs to grow and most commonly used in the kitchen. In whatever culinary creation you concoct in which onions are present, you can substitute chives for a slightly different, milder flavor. The best place to start is by snipping some chives onto a steamy baked potato, smothered in sour cream.

Chives planted in a flowerbed

Features
Other names: fine chives
Parts used: leaves, flowers
Hardiness: zones 3–8

Growing
Chives grow best in **full sun**. The
soil should be **fertile, moist** and
well drained, but chives adapt to
most soil conditions. These plants
are easy to start from seed, but they
do like the soil temperature to stay
above 65°F before they will germinate, so seeds started directly in the
garden are unlikely to sprout before
early summer. To keep the plants
vigorous and healthy, dig up and
divide the clumps every couple of
years, once the flowers have faded in
late summer. If you are not growing
chives for the flowers, then cut the
plant to the ground two or three
times during the growing season to
promote fresh growth from the base.

Tips
Chives are decorative enough to be
included in a mixed or herbaceous
border and can be left to naturalize.
In a herb garden, chives should be
given plenty of space to allow self-
seeding. Chives can also be grown in
containers, allowing you to bring
them in for the winter months.

Recommended
A. schoenoprasum (chives, onion
chives) forms a clump of bright
green, cylindrical leaves. Clusters of
pinky purple flowers are produced
in early and mid-summer. It grows
12–24" tall and 12" wide. **'Forescate'**

*Chives are companion plants to
carrots. When the two are grown
in close proximity, carrots tend to
grow larger.*

Chive butter (above); chives with oregano, thyme and sage (below)

produces pink-purple flowers. **'Grolau'** was developed for indoor use, has thicker leaves and a stronger flavor and produces best when cut frequently. **'Ruby Gem'** has ornamental grey foliage and red flowers. **'Staro'** is a hybrid with thicker leaves ideal for freezing.

A. tuberosum (garlic chives, Chinese chives, Chinese leeks) is a fast-growing species that is very similar to the above species in appearance, but the leaves taste more like a combination of chives and garlic, and are more flat than round. The flowers are white.

Harvesting and Processing

Chives should be used fresh. Dried chives are available but lack flavor. Ideally, snipping chives from the plant is the easiest method of harvest and certainly the most convenient, especially during the growing season. If you've chosen to grow chives indoors, then removing a leaf or two for cooking will not only enhance your meals, but will also encourage the plant to remain dense and full. If you can't grow it indoors, harvest the fresh leaves toward the end of the season, before frost, and mince and freeze with a enough water to fill an ice cube tray. The flowers are best when fresh.

Uses

Mix chives into dips or sprinkle them on salads and baked potatoes. Chives also work well in herb butters, or to flavor cream cheese or other mild, spreadable cheeses. The mild flavor of chives complements and does not overwhelm cheese and cream sauces.

The flowers are perfect for making herbal vinegar, because they not only enhance the flavor of the vinegar, they give it a rosy hue. The flowers can be used as an edible garnish. Gently break them up and use them in combination with the leaves, or on their own.

Chives are said to increase appetite and encourage good digestion. They are also very high in vitamins C and A and calcium, and possess antibacterial and antifungal properties.

A. schoenoprasum (above); chive vinegar (below)

Coriander · Cilantro

Coriandrum

Coriander and cilantro use dates back to biblical times. Today, both are commonly used in a variety of ethnic cuisine, including Mexican, Mediterranean, Cajun and Asian. Coriander is a multi-purpose herb. The leaves, called cilantro, are used in salads, salsas and soups; the seeds, called coriander, are used in pies, chutneys and marmalades. Each has distinct flavors and culinary uses. The seeds have been used in breads and cakes, not only for their flavor but also because of the digestive action the seeds have on breaking down carbohydrates.

Features
Other names: Chinese parsley
Parts used: leaves, seeds
Hardiness: tender annual

Growing
Coriander prefers **full sun**, but tolerates partial shade. The soil should be **fertile, light** and **well drained**. These plants dislike humidity and do best during a dry summer. Preventing the plant from flowering will produce the best leaf development. Deadhead regularly unless you plan to use the flowers.

Tips
Coriander has pungent leaves and is best planted where people will not have to brush past it. It is delightful to behold when in flower, so add a plant or two to your borders and vegetable garden, both for visual appeal and to attract beneficial insects.

Recommended
C. sativum forms a clump of lacy basal foliage above which large, loose clusters of tiny, white flowers are produced. The seeds ripen in late summer and fall. It grows up to 24" tall and 12–18" wide. **'Delfino'** is equally as aromatic and fragrant, but its fine, fern-like foliage gives it a look different from other selections. The leaves taste like parsley with a hint of citrus. The flowers produced by this cultivar are also tasty and a great addition to salads. **'Morocco'** is a fine selection for seed production, while **'Santo'** (Chinese parsley) is very slow to bolt, particularly in regions with hot summers. It is mostly grown for its leaves rather than its seed.

Harvesting and Processing
Harvest the leaves fresh when they are most flavorful. Choose the lower

Coriander flowers and seeds

or older leaves for the strongest flavor unless you prefer a milder flavor. Eat the stems when they are young and tender. Store them in water, stem down, and cover with plastic. Freeze the leaves in ice cube trays for use year-round. The flowers are also flavorful and sweet; pick them as they open. Collect the seeds as soon as they ripen, when the seed turns brown and hardens. Green, unripe seeds can be used for a milder flavor; use them fresh because they do not store well. If you're growing the plants strictly for seed, leave the flowers intact and do not remove too much foliage because the plant will need as much energy to get to the seed stage as possible. Let the seeds dry and store them in an airtight container.

Uses
Use the leaves in soups, stews, spring rolls, salads and salsa. Add toward the end of the cooking time for best flavor. Use the seeds in cakes, cookies, curries, chutneys and pickles. Use the flowers instead of the leaves when a sweeter flavor is desired.

Cress

Lepidium

Cress is not only one plant but a group of botanically unrelated plants grown for their sharp, peppery or mustard-like flavor. Upland cress, *Barbarea verna*, and broadleaf or curly cress, *Lepidium sativum*, are easier to grow than watercress, *Nasturtium officinale*, which requires very moist soil at all times. Most know cress for its use in dainty, crustless finger sandwiches. As yummy as finger sandwiches are, there are many other opportunities to use cress in your culinary repertoire. For our purposes, we're going to focus on one of the selections, *Lepidium sativum*, because of its strong, peppery flavor and ease of growth.

Features
Other names: garden cress, pepperweed, land cress
Parts used: leaves
Hardiness: tender annual

Growing

Cress thrives in **full sun to light shade** in soil that is very **moist, well drained** and of **average fertility**. Sow seed directly in early spring or late summer through fall. Continuous crops will provide you with fresh cress all growing season long. Starting a crop in the middle of summer may cause the plants to produce flowers too quickly without making enough growth to harvest.

Tips

Cress is suitable for the herb garden, but leave enough space for a succession of crops throughout the growing season. Cress can also be grown in containers indoors year-round. Grow cress sprouts by placing seeds on wet paper towels between two layers of plastic or in a plastic container. Mist lightly to keep them moist.

Recommended

L. sativum is a reseeding annual that produces deeply cut, lacy leaves on single, erect stems. Small, almost spherical flowers are produced only three to four weeks after sowing. It grows 6" tall and wide. **'Bubbles'** produces leaves with ruffled edges and blistered surfaces and is quite hot to taste. This cultivar is also slower to bolt than others. **'Greek'** produces flat, dissected leaves that are spicy, sweet and nutty in flavor.

Harvesting and Processing

To harvest, cut back plants by half and they will resprout before flowering. When growing them indoors for use as sprouts (immature plants), use sprouting trays just as you would for other vegetables and herbs. The sprouting trays don't require any soil

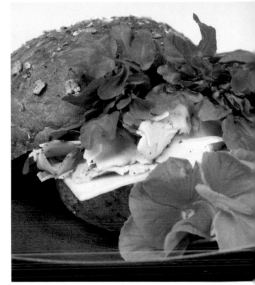
Chicken and cress sandwich

and allow you to harvest the sprouts conveniently all year long. Cress should be used fresh. If you can only grow it outdoors but would like to use it year-round, mince it, combine with water in ice cube trays and freeze for later use.

Uses

Cress is invaluable in salads, sandwiches and garnishes for its spicy flavor and finely curled, nutritious leaves. It is the perfect complement to omelettes and quiche. Cress soup has an unusual and unique flavor. Cress can also serve as a substitute for spinach in dishes where a stronger flavor is required. Most meat dishes will benefit from adding a little cress at the end of cooking.

All cresses are abundant in vitamins and minerals and contain iron, iodine, phosphorus and sulfur.

Curry Plant

Helichrysum

This plant can be a little confusing to some because curry is not the result of one plant. This particular plant is commonly known as the curry plant because the flavor of the leaves is reminiscent of curry powder, which is a combination of many spices, including cumin, coriander, cayenne, cloves, cardamom, turmeric, mustard seed among many others. Curry is also a pretty little ornamental. Its silvery grey color will stand out in a mixed perennial border as well as in decorative containers filled with annuals and herbs. It offers color, aroma and functionality.

Potpourri with dried curry leaves

Features

Parts used: leaves, flowers

Hardiness: zones 7–10, grown as an annual or container plant

Growing

This plant prefers to grow in **full sun** but will tolerate partial shade. The soil should be **well drained** and **poor to moderately fertile**.

Tips

The contrasting colors of curry plant are a complement to just about any container, whether it's a mix of shades or monochromatic. The silver foliage lends itself to areas in the garden that need a little brightening, and the yellow flowers are sure to grab people's attention. Herb gardens are, of course, a common destination for this plant as well.

When prepared as an essential oil, curry is used to augment the flavor of fruit-flavored treats and fragrances.

Recommended

H. italicum is a tender perennial that grows up to 18" tall and 24" wide It is a dense plant, bearing silvery grey, needle-like leaves and clusters of yellow flowers that stand tall above the foliage.

Harvesting and Processing

Use the leaves and flowers fresh through the growing season, or dry them for later use. After pinching off the leaves and flowers, either during the growing season or just before frost for the last harvest of the season, place them in a paper bag to dry, in a cool, dark and dry location.

Uses

H. italicum is not curry, as in the blend of spices known as curry powder, but it has a similar flavor to some curry blends. Add sprigs of this plant to rice and vegetable dishes for a hint of curry flavor.

Dried curry leaves and flowers have a spicy fragrance and insecticidal properties; add them to potpourris and sachets for use in closets and wardrobes.

Dandelion

Taraxacum

Ok, ok, we know what you're thinking. Dandelion? How could I possibly use a weed that's taking over my front yard? Well the time has come to embrace the dandelion. Believe us when we say that it's much easier than consistently fighting it and eventually you'll find yourself touting the benefits of dandelion to all of your friends. Dandelion has been used medicinally for thousands of years. It's also been a staple among certain cuisines for almost as long. Every part of the plant can be used and, clearly, it's easy to grow. All you have to do is get past what we've always been led to believe. Dandelion is an attractive, useful plant, and offers more uses than some common vegetables. If you're willing to try one new thing this year, make it dandelion.

Dried dandelion root

Features
Parts used: leaves, flowers, root
Hardiness: zones 3–10

Growing
Dandelions prefer to grow in **full sun** but will clearly grow in just about any lighting situation. The soil should be **well drained**. Add liberal amounts of **compost** to areas you're sowing if you plan on harvesting the roots. Dandelion readily reseeds itself, but often in places where you'd rather it didn't grow.

Tips
Dandelions can be added to your herb garden or they can be grown in a block or row in your vegetable garden. Dandelions can also be directly sown into containers for harvest closer to the kitchen.

Recommended
T. officinale is a hardy perennial that grows up to 12" tall. It produces long, deeply toothed leaves and deep yellow flowers on tall, hollow stems. The brightly colored flowers quickly change from yellow to fluffy, airy seedheads that are easily taken by the first summer breeze. Dandelions over time develop a deep and somewhat extensive root system, almost taproot-like. **'Thick-leaved Improved'** produces a tender, thicker leaf with less bitterness. **'Verte de Montgomery'** is very similar, but consider that the wild varieties are probably in your yard already, are ripe for the picking and just as tasty.

Dandelion flowers

Harvesting and Processing

A few weeks before harvesting the leaves, cover the plants with a dark, opaque fabric to block out most of the light. This blanches the leaves, which reduces the bitterness. The youngest leaves are the least bitter and most flavorful. The tender leaves can be picked throughout

Dandelion leaves are high in vitamins A and C and contain high levels of potassium, phosphorus, calcium, iron, copper and magnesium.

the growing season. The flowers should be picked when bright, yellow and young. Use the flowers fresh, making sure to remove all of the stem. To prevent the flowers from closing after cutting, place them into a bowl of cold water, taking them out just before eating or serving them.

The roots can be harvested at any time. Chop the dried roots into two-inch pieces and roast at 300° F for about ten minutes. Grind the roasted pieces, adding a quarter teaspoon to your coffee or hot chocolate for a new flavor.

Do not eat dandelions that have been in contact with lawn fertilizers, herbicides or any other synthetic chemical contaminants.

Uses

The leaves are delicious in salads and are a fine substitute for spinach. The flavor of bacon is the perfect complement to dandelion leaves; they also work beautifully in fresh vegetable dishes. Many soups and casseroles benefit from the addition of dandelion leaves.

The crowns are a delicacy when deep-fried, and the roots can be used as a coffee substitute after being roasted and ground.

The flowers can be fermented into wine, used fresh in salads and fried in butter. Young, unopened flower buds are high in protein, are tender and tasty and add a crunch to green salads.

Dandelion leaves and roots (above); dandelion grown with perennials (below)

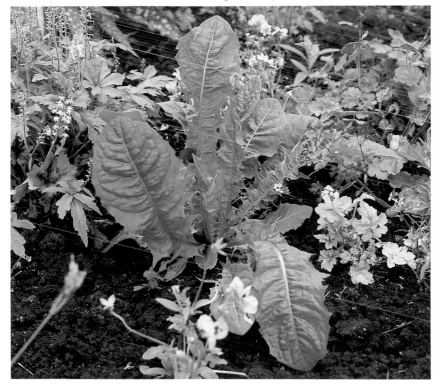

Dill

Anethum

Once known for warding off evil spells, dill is not only part of our folklore throughout the Midwest, but is also a part of our culinary history. Dill leaves and seeds are probably best known for their use as pickling herbs, though they have a wide variety of other culinary uses. The perfect example of a dish we can't imagine without dill is boiled new potatoes straight out of the garden, smothered in butter and sour cream and fresh sprigs of dill. Dill is another herb that is incredibly easy to grow, requiring nothing more than a little space. The rest will take care of itself.

The popular Scandinavian dish gravalax *is made by marinating a fillet of salmon with oil, salt, sugar and the leaves and seeds of dill.*

Fresh dill stems (top), dried dill leaves (left) and dill seeds (right)

Features
Other names: dillweed
Parts used: leaves, seeds
Hardiness: annual

Growing
Dill grows best in **full sun** in a
sheltered location out of strong
winds. The soil should be of **poor
to average fertility, moist** and **well
drained.** Sow seeds every couple of
weeks in spring and early summer
to ensure a regular supply of leaves.
Plants should not be grown near
fennel because they will cross-
pollinate and the seeds will lose
their distinct flavors.

*Dill turns up frequently in
historical records as both a culinary
and a medicinal herb. It was used
by the Egyptians and Romans and
is mentioned in the Bible.*

Tips
With its feathery leaves, dill is an
attractive addition to a mixed bed or
border. It can be included in a vegetable garden, but does well in any sunny
location. It also attracts predatory
insects to the garden.

Recommended
A. graveolens forms a clump of
feathery, finely cut, aromatic foliage.
Clusters of yellow flowers are borne
at the tops of sturdy stems. It grows
2–5' tall and 12" or more wide.
'Bouquet' produces high seed and
leaf yields. **'Dukat'** also known as
tetra dill, is grown for its abundant
foliage that doesn't resemble dill foliage as you currently know it. This
selection produces leaves and seeds
that lend a distinctive flavor to pickles, breads, dips and spreads. **Var.
'Fernleaf'** produces high yields of
leaves in a dwarf form and is slow to
bolt. **'Hercules'** is an extremely tall
selection with a dense, leafy habit.

Flowering dill (above and opposite page)

'**Mammoth**' produces sparse foliage and quickly goes to seed, producing large seed heads. It is one of the best for pickling. '**Vierling**' is the best selection for ornamental use. It bears steel blue foliage and chartreuse blooms with strong stems and early flowers. The leaves can be used as they would normally.

Harvesting and Processing

Fresh dill is by far the best, but when the growing season ends, it's time to remove the foliage from the stems for drying. Dried dill can be as flavorful as fresh when the leafy stalks are cut before the flowerheads appear. Spread the stalks on a wire rack in a shady, cool location until dry. Gently rub the dried leaves from the stalks into airtight containers. Fresh dill leaves can also be frozen for later use by finely chopping them, mixing them with water and pouring the mixture into an ice cube tray.

Collect ripened seeds in the fall as soon as the seed begins to fall from the seedheads. Remove the heads, spread them onto a tray and leave them in the sun to dry. When dry, gently shake the seeds from the heads into airtight containers.

Dill-flavored cream cheese (above)

Uses

Dill not only tastes delicious but it also helps the digestion of certain foods, including cabbage, bread and cooked root vegetables. Mix a little into your cottage cheese or cream cheese. Dill seems made for egg and potato dishes, and it also works well in salad dressings, sauces and most rice, fish and lamb dishes. This herb is used in the cuisines of Scandinavia, the Middle East, the Mediterranean, Thailand, Vietnam and Laos, among others.

The seeds have been used to pickle baby cucumbers, carrots and cabbage for generations.

Elderberry

Sambucus

Elderberries have what we all want in a shrub—flowers (often fragrant), berries, interesting foliage and a practical use for almost every part of the plant. Cultivars with varied leaf characteristics and habits are bringing a new level of awareness to this group of plants. To keep them looking tidy, most species should be pruned.

Fresh and dried elderberry

Features

Other names: elder
Parts used: flowers, berries
Hardiness: zones 3–9

Growing

Elderberries grow well in **full sun** or **partial shade**. Cultivars grown for burgundy or black leaf color develop the best color in full sun, while cultivars with yellow leaf color develop the best color in light or partial shade. The soil should be of **average fertility, moist** and **well drained**. These plants tolerate dry soil once established.

Though elderberries do not require pruning, they can become scraggly and untidy if ignored. They will tolerate even severe pruning. Plants can be cut back to within a couple of buds of the ground in early spring. This treatment controls the spread of these vigorous growers and encourages the best foliage color on specimens grown for this purpose.

Plants cut right back to the ground will not flower or produce fruit that season. If you desire flowers and fruit as well as good foliage color, remove only one-third to one-half of the growth in early spring. Fertilize or apply a layer of compost after pruning to encourage strong new growth.

Tips

Elderberries can be used in shrub or mixed borders, in natural woodland gardens or next to ponds or other water features. Plants with interesting or colorful foliage can be used as specimen plants or to create focal points in the garden.

Elderberry fruit attracts birds to the garden.

S. nigra 'Aureomarginata'

Recommended

S. canadensis (*S. nigra* subsp. *canadensis;* American elderberry) is a shrub about 12' tall, with an equal spread. White, mid-summer flowers are followed by dark purple berries. A widespread native across the eastern and central U.S., this species is generally found growing in damp ditches and alongside rivers and streams. '**Aurea**' has yellow foliage and red fruit. '**Goldfinch**' has finely cut, yellow foliage (Zones 4–9).

S. nigra (*S. nigra* subsp. *nigra;* European elderberry, black elderberry) is a large shrub that can grow 15' tall and wide. The yellowish white to creamy white, early summer flowers are followed by purple-black fruit. BLACK BEAUTY ('Gerda') has dark foliage that gets blacker as the season progresses. The flowers are pink. It grows 8–12' tall, with an equal spread. '**Laciniata**' has deeply dissected leaflets that give the shrub a feathery appearance. It grows up to 10' tall and wide. '**Madonna**' has dark green foliage with wide, irregular, yellow margins. '**Pulverulenta**' has unusually dark green and white mottled foliage. It grows slower than other cultivars but reaches 10' in height and spread (Zones 4–8).

Harvesting and Processing

Pick the flowers soon after they open and the berries once they ripen or are fully colored. Rinse the flowers with water before eating them to remove all insects. Strain out all seeds, which contain toxins, and consume the berries sparingly because the fruit has a laxative effect.

S. canadensis with fruit just beginning to form (above); *S. canadensis* with flower and fruit (below)

Uses

Both the flowers and the fruit can be used to make wine. The berries are also popular for pies and jelly. The raw berries are marginally edible but not palatable and can cause stomach upset, particularly in children. Cook the berries before eating them. Try them in place of blueberries in pies, scones or muffins. The berries can also be made into jams and jellies. Elderflower fritters, fresh flowerheads dipped in batter, fried and dusted with sugar are tasty. Fresh or dried flowers can be added to desserts and sorbets, or to fresh or cooked gooseberries and stewed fruits.

Cosmetically, elder flowers have been used in a variety of toiletries, including a cream said to reducing the evidence of wrinkles by tightening the skin.

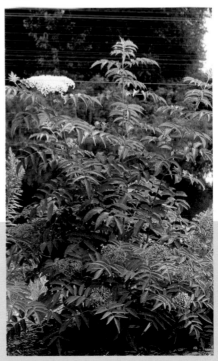

Note that **not all elderberries are edible**. The two recommended species listed here are safe, but others may not be. The rule of thumb is that red-fruited species are poisonous and black- or blue-fruited species are edible, but only when ripe and cooked.

Fennel

Foeniculum

Fennel has been part of history for thousands of years in one capacity or other. Herbalists have touted the benefits of this plant for its healing capabilities, and cooks have used fennel both as a vegetable and herb in a variety of ways. This plant even has cosmetic qualities that are said to smooth wrinkles and lines and refresh tired eyes. Once you've tried cooking with fennel, you'll find yourself searching for more and more ways to use this wonderfully tasty and aromatic herb.

F. vulgare 'Bronze' in bloom

Features

Other names: common fennel, sweet fennel
Parts used: leaves, bulb or swollen stem base, seeds
Hardiness: zones 4–9

Growing

Fennel grows best in **full sun**. The soil should be **average to fertile, moist** and **well drained**. Avoid planting fennel near dill and coriander, because cross-pollination reduces seed production and makes the seed flavor of each less distinct. Fennel is also a poor garden companion to caraway, tomatoes, kohlrabi and dwarf beans. Fennel easily self-sows.

Tips

Fennel is an attractive addition to a mixed bed or border, and it can be included in a vegetable garden. It also attracts pollinators and predatory insects to the garden, and is a food source for swallowtail caterpillars.

Fennel can be grown in containers, too. If you're only after young, tender leaves, then crowd the pot with at least six plants. If you would also like to harvest the stalks then reduce that number to three. Marigolds and nasturtiums are the perfect companions in containers and equally as useful. Fennel can also be grown in containers indoors but only for the leaves as its unlikely to produce seeds or bulb.

Recommended

F. vulgare is a short-lived perennial that forms clumps of loose, feathery foliage. Clusters of small, yellow flowers are borne in late summer. The seeds ripen in fall. This species is primarily grown for its seeds and leaves. It grows 2–6' tall and 12–24" wide. **Var.** *azoricum* (Florence fennel, finocchio) is a biennial that forms a large, edible bulb at the stem base. This variety is grown for its stems, leaves and bulb. The licorice-flavored bulb is popular raw in salads,

F. vulgare (above); *F. vulgare* 'Bronze' (below)

cooked in soups or stews and roasted like other root vegetables. **Var. *dulce*** (sweet fennel) bears green-brown seeds. **'Purpureum'** (*rubrum*, 'Atropurpureum', var. *dulce* 'Purpureum', bronze fennel) is similar in appearance to the species but has bronzy purple foliage. This cultivar is usually sold as an ornamental, but its parts are entirely edible.

Harvesting and Processing

The leaves can be harvested all season long, as well as the stems. They're most flavorful when used fresh; drying is not recommended. At the end of the season, before hard frost, cut the stems either to the ground or to the bulb. Discard the tough stems and chop the rest, add a little water to the mix and fill an ice cube tray or two with the mixture for freezing.

The bulb should be used fresh as a vegetable. To harvest, cut plant at soil level in the fall or when it appears large enough for cooking.

To collect the seeds, remove the seedheads before the seeds start to fall off. It's important to dry them properly before storage to prevent them from getting musty.

Uses

Because of the seductive scent and flavor of licorice, fennel is the perfect complement to certain cuisines and dishes, including fish. All parts can be used in cooking, whether its the leaves and stems for dressings, salads or vegetable dishes; the seeds in pastries, pasta and sauces; or the bulb as a root vegetable, grated into salads or smothered in a white sauce. The leaves and seeds are tasty in herbal vinegars and herbed butters.

Fennel tea made with fennel seeds (above), young fennel and tomato plants (below)

Fennel tea, made by steeping the seeds in boiling water, helps to settle an upset stomach, aids digestion and prevents heartburn and constipation.

Steeping a compress in the tea and placing it on the eyelids will ease inflammation or puffy eyes. A strong fennel infusion combined with honey and buttermilk makes a great cleansing lotion for the face. Replace the buttermilk with yogurt and you have the perfect revitalizing face mask.

Crafters appreciate the versatility of this herb as well. The essential oil is commonly used in hand made soaps and fragrances.

Fenugreek

Trigonella

This herb isn't nearly as well known as some others, such as dill, but it's worth experimenting with. The dried leaves have been used to flavor root dishes in Middle Eastern cooking for generations. Fenugreek is frequently used in Indian cuisine to flavor curries. The leaves are also an important ingredient in tandoori marinades, while the seeds are part of specific curry blends, such as the distinctive vindaloo. Fenugreek is principally a cleansing, soothing herb; its sprouts have a variety of tasty uses, too, and are said to have tonic properties.

Features

Parts used: leaves, seeds, sprouts
Hardiness: annual

Growing

Fenugreek prefers to grow in a location with **full sun. Well drained, moist, fertile soil** is best. The seed can be sown in early spring and will germinate in cold soils.

Tips

This herb is useful and attractive in a herb garden, but it can also adorn a mixed bed or border. It can also be grown in a decorative container as a specimen or mixed with other herbs, perennials and annuals. When planted as a specimen, it can be brought indoors in the fall, where it will be at your fingertips for easy harvest.

Recommended

T. foenum-graecum is an erect annual that grows 18–24" tall. It produces deeply lobed leaves reminiscent of clover but more elongated. Pale yellow flowers emerge in midsummer followed by a curved pod that comes to a point resembling a beak. Each fruit contains up to 20 light brown, fragrant seeds.

Harvesting and Processing

If you're using the leaves to cook with, pick them once they're fairly large. Use fresh leaves because drying is not recommended. Finely chopping some leaves, combining them with a little water in ice cube trays and freezing them is a reliable way to stretch out your supply of fenugreek through the winter months.

If growing the plant for the seed, allow the plant to flower and set fruit.

Fenugreek stems (above); fenugreek seeds (opposite)

Collect the ripened pods after the first few seeds begin to fall from them. Remove the pods and spread onto trays in a dry location. When dry, shake the seeds from the pods and store them in an airtight containers.

Uses

High in vitamin, mineral and iron content, fenugreek leaves are cooked as a vegetable, especially in Indian cuisine. Eat fresh fenugreek sprouts as a snack, juiced with vegetables, added to sandwiches and salads and mixed with potato salad and other root vegetables. The sprouts can be used as a garnish or added to soups, rice and pasta dishes and stir-fries just before serving. Do not cook sprouts because they go mushy.

The seeds are frequently used in curry powder blends. They can also be added to pastries, marinades, pickles and chutneys. Roasted seeds can be used as a coffee substitute.

Garlic and Leeks

Allium

Garlic and leeks are not only incredibly aromatic and flavorful but nutritious, too. Garlic is high in vitamins A, B and C, copper, manganese, iron, sulfur and calcium, so it is an important herb for anyone and everyone. Garlic also has its place in history. Garlic juice was used in World War I to prevent wounds from becoming septic. Classic writers such as Pliny, Horace, Virgil and later Chaucer and Shakespeare have recorded its use. It was also known to Homer, and I'm not talking about Mr. Simpson, either. The Romans, Greeks and Egyptians all knew of its excellent properties, just as we do today. Maybe the old adage should be "eating a clove of garlic a day keeps the doctor away."

Mature garlic plants with straw mulch (above); garlic bulbs (opposite)

Features
Parts used: bulb
Hardiness: zones 3–8

Growing
Garlic and leeks should be grown in an area with **full to partial sun**. **Well drained, light, alkaline soils** are best.

Separate garlic bulbs into cloves. The cloves or bulblets should be planted with skins intact in early spring, as soon as the frost is out of the ground. Plant cloves pointed end up and root end down, 2" deep and 6" apart. Elephant garlic cloves can be planted a little further apart. It's best to use garlic sets from the garden center for planting. Use only the largest cloves from the bulb. You can also plant cloves in the fall for harvest the following summer or fall. Remove the flowers as they emerge to redirect the energy back into the formation of the bulb. Some have better success planting in late September or early October for harvest

the following July and August. If you find that your garlic is just too small when planted in the spring, leave it in the ground until the following year to harvest. Experiment and practice to find what works for you.

Leeks should be planted as early as possible in the spring, because the seedlings aren't sensitive to light frosts. The earlier you plant it, the thicker the stems will be. Leek seed can be started indoors and transplanted as soon as you can get into the garden.

Tips
Garlic and leeks aren't really ornamental, particularly when you remove the flowers to keep the plants' energy in the bulbs and stems. They could be planted in a narrow border as an architectural element, but they are often planted in a vegetable or herb garden for harvest in mind. Both garlic and leeks can be grown in a container if there is an unheated garage or shed to store them in over the

Garlic bulbs and cloves (above);
Leeks (below and right)

winter. Be sure that the soil is moist before it is left to freeze and check it from time to time throughout the winter so it isn't allowed to dry out. Move the container outdoors in early spring and it will begin to sprout once the days are warm enough. In warmer regions, a container planted with garlic can remain outdoors.

Recommended

A. ampeloprasum (var. *ampeloprasum*, elephant garlic, Russian garlic, Levant garlic) is not a "true" garlic species. It is more closely related to onions and leeks. This species produces giant bulbs that look and taste like garlic, but milder. The bulbs are much larger than *A. sativum*, consisting of an average of 5–6 large cloves. **'American Flag'** is a sweet and mild-flavored leek that is very cold hardy. **'Giant Carentan'** is an old French selection that produces a very mild flavor and is extremely tender. **Var. porrum** (leeks) resemble a thick, overgrown scallion with thicker, strap-like leaves. The flavor is closer to an onion but milder. **'Varna'** is a tall, thick leek that is a great substitute

Roasted garlic makes a great spread for toast.

for spring onions in salads or when lightly steamed.

A. *sativum* (common garlic) starts as a bulb, or a tight cluster of bulbs. Deep below the soil's surface, the cluster produces a sprout of growth that reaches the soil's surface displaying grass-like leaves 12–24" tall. A rigid, tall and straw-like flowerstalk emerges from the center of the leaves, topped with a rounded cluster of purple-tinted, tiny flowers that form into a globular shape. Garlic is split into hardneck and softneck subspecies. Hardneck varieties tend to be more intensely flavored. Softneck varieties tend to be less intense, store better and are used to create beautiful garlic braids.

Harvesting and Processing

Once half of the foliage of the garlic plant has died back in mid-summer, dig the bulbs up carefully with a garden fork. Leaving the bulbs in the ground until all of the foliage dies back will result in shattered bulbs, which are difficult to remove from the soil. Leave the bulbs on the ground for a few days, but only if it's warm and dry.

Shake the soil loose, cut the spent leaves 2–3" above each bulb and allow the bulbs to dry completely before storing. Store only in containers that have good air circulation, such as garlic pots and wire baskets, or braid the stems to hang in a pantry.

Dig leeks in late fall. Transfer them, with stems intact and roots covered in soil, into a box as if you were transplanting them into the box. Store the leeks in a cool location and remove stalks as needed.

Uses

Use garlic fresh or roasted to flavor a wide variety of dishes. It can be used whole, chopped, minced or sliced. Each clove packs a punch, so a few go a long way.

Leeks are often cooked into soups, stews or casseroles. They are also used fresh, either together with other onion and garlic species or on their own, for a mild onion flavor.

Garlic is effective for lowering blood sugar levels and cholesterol, aids in curing fungal infections and boosts immunity, helping to ward off the common cold and flu.

German Chamomile

Matricaria

You, too, can grow your own crop of medicinal chamomile, just in time for those moments when you need to slow things down and calm your frazzled nerves. This delicate-looking plant is also frequently used in a variety of toiletries and bath products and although the culinary uses are few, they are fun.

Features

Other names: chamomile, scented mayweed
Parts used: flowers
Hardiness: annual

Growing

German chamomile prefers to grow in locations with **full sun to light shade**. **Well drained, moist** and **light soil** that is neutral to slightly acidic is best. Starting with young plants is best, but you can also try sowing seed into small peat pots for transplanting later on or transplanting seedlings.

Dried German chamomile mixed with honey, oats and water to make a facial mask

Tips

This aromatic herb is perfectly suited to herb gardens. It will self-seed around the garden, but it's easy to remove from where it is not wanted. Leave a few plants in the garden to produce and sow seed for next year.

Do not confuse *M. recutita* with a different plant commonly called Roman chamomile, *Chamaemelum nobile*. Its essential oils are completely different, and inferior to German chamomile.

Recommended

M. recutita is a sweetly scented annual or biennial. It produces branched stems and finely divided leaves. Daisy-like flowers are borne from early summer to fall. It grows 6–24" tall and 4–12" wide.

Harvesting and Processing

Harvest the flowers when they are fully open. Use them fresh, or preserve them by drying or freezing. To dry, spread the flowers on a screen or sheet of paper until dry and store in a dark, airtight container. To best preserve the flowers' volatile oils, particularly storing them for long periods, freeze the flowers in airtight containers. Drying the flowers will cause the oils to rapidly diminish.

Uses

This and other species of chamomile are used to make a tea that is often used as a sedative, as well as a digestive aid. It's also very tasty to flavor fruit dishes, and to cream or light cheeses. A few whole flowers sprinkled onto a salad are an edible garnish.

This herb has also been used in cosmetics and crafts for generations. It's not uncommon to find it as an ingredient in facial oils, floral water and compresses. Crafters use the flowers in potpourri, dried arrangements, garlands and sachets for scenting closets and drawers. Combine it with bran, honey and boiling water for a facial mask; create a conditioning rinse for your hair by combining it with with a handful of scented geranium leaves and boiling water. Once cooled, both concoctions are a refreshing treat for your skin and hair. Throw a sachet filled with any type of chamomile into a bath for a soothing soak.

Ginger Root

Zingiber

Most people think of ginger as a tropical plant that couldn't possibly be grown in their own backyards, but you can grow it and year round regardless of what zone you live in. This is where container culture becomes a true blessing because it allows people in cold climates to grow plants they couldn't ordinarily. In fact this is a project you can get the kids involved in because if nothing else, growing ginger is fun and interesting, and will reward you with its sweet, spicy flavor and aroma.

Features

Other names: ginger
Parts used: rhizomes or root
Hardiness: tender tuber grown as an annual or container plant

Grated ginger root

Growing

When grown outdoors, ginger root should be in the sunniest spot available, preferably **full sun** if possible. While indoors, it should be positioned in the brightest location or grown under a grow light assembly. Grow in a **light soil** with **adequate drainage** and **fertility**. Add compost into the mixture to improve its richness.

Select a container that is at least 12" deep. Cut the fresh root into pieces for several plants or plant the root whole. Set the root just below the surface of the soil mix. Set the pot in a warm and sunny location, watering only sparingly until growth emerges. Water thoroughly after

shoots appear. Mist occasionally or frequently, depending on your region, to increase the humidity. The pot can also be placed onto a pebble tray filled with water or placed in a room with a humidifier. The container can be put outdoors in a sunny location after the risk of frost has passed. Make sure to bring it back indoors long before fall frost. It will go dormant during the winter months, slowing down until the day length increases in spring. Repot it annually to accommodate its new growth.

To cook with ginger, scrape or peel the skin from the fibrous flesh using the edge of a teaspoon. Once peeled, ginger can be sliced, chopped, minced, pressed or grated, depending on the recipe.

Z. officinale (above); dug up roots (below)

Tips

Containers of ginger root are easily displayed on decks, balconies, porches, steps and around the pool. The foliar display will remind you of tropical destinations, perfect for an exotic-themed garden design.

Recommended

Z. officinale is a perennial, tropical herb that is grown primarily for its root. It produces bright green, thick stems with long, strap-like foliage and exotic yellow flowers with hints of green. It can reach 3–4' heights but may take years to get there.

Harvesting and Processing

A year after planting, once the plant is well established, the roots can be dug up. The newer, more tender roots that have developed over the year are far more flavorful than the older ones. Cut the stems and roots away. The roots will keep in the refrigerator for three weeks or more. The root can also be dried, ground into ginger powder, and stored in

Candied ginger cubes

airtight containers. Ginger root freezes beautifully when placed into a freezer bag and will last for months and months.

Uses

Ginger root can be used fresh or dried and ground. A wide variety of ethnic cuisines use ginger root fre quently as a trademark flavor. Japanese, Thai and Chinese cooking often require a slice of ginger to enhance the fresh flavors of vegetables and meats. Sliced and grated ginger is a pungent addition to stir-fries, chutneys and confectionary. Ginger can be used in baked goods, including spicy cookies like gingerbread. It can also be candied for a treat.

Essential oil of ginger is used in fragrances and can be used to scent handmade soaps, lotions or spent potpourri. The oil can also be added to massage oils to ease rheumatic pain and aching joints.

Ginger root has antiseptic properties, and helps to settle an upset stomach, or to treat indigestion, menstrual pain and travel sickness.

Ginger root is also known as adrak, gin, khing, jeung *and* shoga *in other cultures around the world.*

Heliotrope

Heliotropium

Heliotrope was introduced into cultivation in Europe in 1757, and by the 19th century, it was used extensively in gardens all over the world. It was nicknamed the "cherry pie plant" because the fragrance produced by the rich purple flowers is reminiscent of freshly baked cherry pie. That fragrance is often used as a note in perfumes even today. The scent has also been compared to vanilla, almond and baby powder. Even for the scent-challenged, heliotrope is a must-have plant and a striking contrast to many flowers, especially those with warmer colors. The end result is one color playing off another, bringing all of heliotrope's best attributes forward.

Features

Other names: cherry pie plant
Parts used: flowers
Hardiness: evergreen subshrub grown as an annual or container plant

Growing

Heliotrope grows best in **full sun**. The soil should be **fertile, rich in organic matter, moist** and **well drained**. Although overwatering will kill heliotrope, if left to dry to the point of wilting, the plant will be slow to recover.

Heliotrope is sensitive to cold weather, so plant it out after all danger of frost has passed. Protect it with newspaper or a floating row cover if an unexpected late frost occurs. Container-grown plants can be brought indoors at night if frost is expected.

Tips

Grow heliotrope in containers or in beds near windows and patios where the wonderful scent of the flowers can be enjoyed. Create a tree form, or standard, by pinching off the lower branches as the plant grows until it reaches the height you desire; then pinch the top to encourage the plant to bush out. Create a shorter, bushier form by pinching all the tips that develop to encourage the plant to bush out at ground level.

Heliotrope can be grown indoors. A plant may survive for years if kept outdoors all summer and indoors all winter in a cool, bright room.

Recommended

H. arborescens is a low, bushy shrub that is usually treated as an annual. It grows 18–24" tall, with an equal spread. Large clusters of purple, blue or white, scented flowers are produced all summer. Some new cultivars are not as strongly scented as the species. **'Alba'** is a white selection with a strong, heady scent and **'Atlantic'** produces deep purple-blue, vanilla-scented flower clusters.

Heliotrope grows well in containers.

'Black Beauty' has deep, dark flowers and **'Blue Wonder'** is a compact plant that was developed for heavily scented flowers. Plants grow up to 16" tall with dark purple flowers. **'Dwarf Marine'** ('Mini Marine') is a compact, bushy plant with fragrant, purple flowers. It grows 8–12" tall and also makes a good houseplant for a bright location. **'Fragrant Delight'** is an older cultivar with royal purple, intensely fragrant flowers. It can reach a height of 4' if grown as a standard. **'Marine'** has violet blue flowers and grows about 18" tall.

Harvesting and Processing

Pick the flowers throughout the blooming cycle and use fresh or dry them on screens, in paper bags or in bunches, and hang on drying racks out of direct light.

Uses

Use the flowers in soaps, lotions, hair rinses, sachets, potpourri and herbal pillows. The dried or fresh flowers work well in floral arrangements and blend beautifully with scented geraniums and any yellow-flowered plant as a contrast in color.

Hops
Humulus

Hops isn't only for the garden aficionado; it deserves appreciation for its valuable and enjoyable versatility. Hops has been used medicinally for treatment of insomnia, skin infections, nervous tension and anxiety. Aside from its ornamental value in the garden, hops has been one of the main ingredients for brewing beer and has been since the 9th century, replacing bitter herbs such as *Glechoma hederacea*. The aromatic flowers have uses of their own, in fragrances and rejuvenating bath and hair treatments. Considering this plant's hardiness and vigor, gardeners at any level of gardening expertise can grow hops successfully. If you sit still long enough you can even see it grow.

Features
Parts used: leaves, shoots, female flowers, oil
Hardiness: zones 3–8

Growing

Hops prefers **full to partial sun**. The soil should be **moist, moderately fertile, organically rich** and **well drained**. Divide in spring or fall, or propagate by stem cuttings in spring. If you plan to use hops to make beer, it's easiest to begin with female starter plants because beer is made using the unpollinated female flowers. In regions with cold wet winters, shield hops from moisture by growing it in large containers that can be stored in a garage or shed.

Tips

Hops is most often trained as a climber on trellises, arbors, a variety of fencing, old trees, obelisks or along the side of a building. It can be left to crawl along the ground around shrubs and trees as well. In the Midwest, hops will die to the ground each fall but return with vigor the following summer.

Recommended

H. lupulus vigorously produces hairy vines, densely covered in coarse, deep green, toothed leaves. Fragrant green flowers emerge in early summer that change to tan with age. This vine can reach 25–30' heights, once established, in one season.

'**Aureus**' is strictly ornamental. It bears golden yellow foliage and reaches a mature height of 20'.

If you make beer, try any of the following species: the excellent, all-purpose '**Cascade**'; '**Haller-tauer**,' which is used in German lagers and has a pleasant aroma; '**Magnum**,' a selection that produces a very high yield of hops that have a "middle flavor"; '**Mount Hood**,'

H. lupulus 'Aureus,' or golden hops

which also has a medium bitterness and a mild flavor that works best for Bavarian-style lagers; '**Nugget**,' which has a strong bitter flavor best suited to stouts and ales; or '**Willamette**,' which has a spicy aroma.

Harvesting and Processing

Pick male flowers as required and collect female flowers in the fall. The flowers are ready when they've turned light brown, have a papery feel and are free of dark spots. Air dry the flowers on screens or in a 300° F oven. Once dry, store the flowers in airtight containers and use for up to one year. The longer they're left, the more bitter they may become.

Uses

Cut and cook the young shoots that appear in spring and summer just as you would prepare asparagus. Harvest the flowers to make beer.

Add the dried flowers to arrangements, potpourri and sachets or make into garlands. Use the essential oil of hops in handmade toiletries.

To relieve insomnia, tuck a small sachet filled with hops flowers into your pillow or between your pillow and its case (a dream pillow).

Horseradish

Armoracia

Can you imagine using horseradish to brush your teeth? And you thought mouthwash was strong. Because its volatile oils block the bacterial growth that causes dental plaque, this root was once an addition to the morning repertoire hundreds of years ago. You're thankful for the makers of toothpaste now, aren't you? The medicinal value of this root has been noted throughout history, in the treatment of headaches, stuffy sinuses and bronchial infections. Today, we're more accustomed to using horseradish as a condiment with our roast beef, but this herb has much more to offer.

Features
Other names: redcole, stingnose
Parts used: roots, leaves
Hardiness: zones 3–8

Growing
Horseradish grows best in **full sun.**
The soil should be **well drained,
light, moist** and **of average fertility.**
The roots' flavor can be compro-
mised if horseradish is left to grow
in soil that is too wet, too rich or too
fertilized. Horseradish is easiest to
start with a root cutting available
from your local garden center, but
you can also start it from seed. Dormant roots can be planted out in
early spring, spaced at least 12" apart.

Tips
The broad, tall leaves and stems of
horseradish complement plants with
finely dissected foliage and delicate
flowers. It looks best planted at the
back of a border, but works well in
any vegetable or herb garden.

Recommended
A. rusticana is a very hardy perennial
that grows 1–4' tall and 24–36" wide.
The root can grow 24" deep. It produces long-stalked, tall leaves and
fleshy, cream-colored roots in small
clusters. White flowers on drooping
stems are produced in early to mid-
summer. **'Variegata'** produces variegated or marbled leaves with creamy
markings.

Harvesting and Processing
The roots can be harvested throughout the growing season but are most
commonly dug up after a hard frost
in fall. Fall is the best time to harvest
the root because it's had the growing
season to produce young flesh, which
is less woody than an older root.

A. rusticana 'Variegata'

Roots left in the soil will resprout the
following year, so if this is not to your
liking, dig them out. Otherwise, leave
one parent plant behind for propagation the following spring.

Once harvested, store the root in
the refrigerator. The pungent fumes
from freshly cut horseradish root are
the result of oxidation.

Uses
Mix ground or grated roots with vinegar, salt, sugar, dill and low fat cream
cheese to make a sauce similar to the
prepared horseradish you find in the
grocery store. Vinegar combined with
the grated root preserves it for later
use and subdues its pungency. Horseradish sauce is typically served with
meats such as beef, chicken and hard-
boiled eggs; it can also spice up red
sauces or give sandwiches a little kick.
Horseradish is rich in calcium, magnesium and vitamin C; it also contains sodium and has antibiotic
qualities, useful to preserve food.

The youngest leaves are mild and
yummy in salads and sandwiches.

Hyssop
Hyssopus

Much folklore is connected to this fragrant herb. The Romans were said to
have used it in healing practices and ceremonies. Monks would plant hyssop
as a border hedge in their gardens for its holy and medicinal properties, often
in temple purification ceremonies. Today it is a valued herb but for different
reasons. As a companion plant, it will repel (and some claim kill) whitefly
from your cabbage plants, and, when planted close to grape vines, may
increase fruit production. Even if you never use hyssop for anything but
its ornamental value, you'll still find it a surefire winner.

Features
Parts used: leaves, flowers
Hardiness: zones 4–9

Growing

Hyssop grows well in **fertile, well drained soil in full sun**. Begin with a starter plant rather than sowing from seed, especially in zones colder than 6. Dig up the rootball in early spring every few years to cut away and remove the old woody crown.

Tips

Hyssop's lovely pink, purple and blue flowers fill the color void in mid-summer, perfectly complementing to warm-colored flowers and foliage in a mixed border of perennials and shrubs. This shrubby plant is also very attractive to bees and pollinating insects. It also makes a great container plant for window boxes, and for locations on a hot deck or balcony.

Recommended

H. officinalis is a dwarf, semi-evergreen, 24" woody plant that produces tall spikes carrying narrow, mid-green leaves and topped with funnel-shaped, two-lipped, dark blue-purple flower spikes. The flowers emerge in midsummer and last until early fall. **'Albus'** produces white flowers and **subsp.** *aristatus* is a more compact selection of the species. **'Grandiflora'** produces large flowers, **'Purpurescens'** ('Rubra') has deep reddish flowers and **'Roseus'** bears medium pink flower spikes. **'Sissinghurst'** has a dwarf growth habit. The **Nectar Series** is also available, with flowers in a variety of cool colors. **'Nectar'** is an early flowering selection and highly fragrant; **'Blue Nectar'** has bluish flowers; **'Rose Nectar'** bears pink blossoms; and **'White Nectar'** has white flowers.

Hyssop oil and fragrance

Harvesting and Processing

Cut stem tips as the flowers are newly opening. Dry them preferably in a slow oven (300° F) or in bunches hung in a dry, cool location. Once dry, strip the flowers from the stems and store in an airtight container, in a cool, dark cupboard. Store dried leaves separately, in airtight containers for later use.

Uses

Hyssop flowers are delicious and add a bit of color when tossed into a green salad. In small amounts, the leaves aid in the digestion of fatty foods. Hyssop has a bitter flavor with a hint of mint that goes well with meat dishes, gravy, stuffing, stews. Use it in sausages, fruit pies and sugar syrup for sprinkling over fresh fruit.

Its fragrant oil is used in perfumes. The oil and leaves have antiseptic properties, and can be added to boiling water to create a steam bath to treat acne. Try a drop or two of hyssop oil in a bath for a refreshing treat.

During pregnancy, no form of hyssop should be taken internally.

Jasmine

Jasminum

Jasmine is a vigorously growing vine with intensely scented blossoms. It is part of a genus consisting of approximately 200 species. Because of jasmine's vigorous growth habit, some people prefer to grow it in a space where it can grow freely without constraints and in the conditions it requires to thrive. Ideally, the best place to grow jasmine indoors is in a conservatory, greenhouse, atrium or sunroom, but it can grow well in a bright, sunny location in a more typical home environment. It's easy to train jasmine onto any kind of support structure as long as it's pruned to control its size.

J. nudiflorum (above), mainly an ornamental variety

Parts used: flowers
Hardiness: tropical, hardiness zone
varies with species, grown as a
container plant

Growing

Outdoors, jasmine prefers to grow in
a **sunny but sheltered location**, in
fertile, well-drained soil. Indoors as
a houseplant, jasmine should be
grown in **moderate to bright light**
with **some direct sunlight**. The **soil-
based potting mix** should be kept
moist during the growing season.
Allow the surface of the mix to dry
out slightly between waterings in
winter, but mist the foliage regularly.
When grown as a houseplant, set it
outdoors for the summer and bring
it indoors long before the first fall
frost. Propagate it by cuttings and
repot it in the spring.

Tips

Grow jasmine in a large container
with a suitable support. Prune it
back once or twice annually to contain its size and prevent it from
becoming top heavy and straggly.

All parts are poisonous if ingested.

Recommended

J. mesnyi (*J. primulinum*, primrose jasmine) produces non-twining stems
clothed in leaves made up of three leaflets each. The bright yellow, unscented
flowers are semi-double, 1–1 ½" across
with 6 or more petals. Cultivars are
available with double flowers that
emerge where the leaves meet the
stems.

J. nitidum is a sun-loving, vining jasmine that is usually pruned to form a
dense "shrub." The buds are a deep purple and some of the purple coloration is
retained in the sepals when the very fragrant blooms are fully open (Zone 9).

J. officinale (white jasmine) is a climber
with divided leaves and loose sprays of
scented, white flowers. The flowers have
long, tubular throats that open into
five-petalled, star-shaped "faces."
'Affine' blooms more profusely than
the species and has larger flowers with
pink exteriors. **'Aureum'** has yellow,
variegated leaves and white flowers.

The fragrant flowers of *J. nudiflorum* (above)

J. x stephanense over a porch entrance (above); *J. nitidum*, a very fragrant, vining jasmine (below)

J. polyanthum (pink jasmine, Chinese jasmine) is similar to *J. officinale* but bears pink buds that open into white, starry, fragrant flowers. The twining stems are covered in five to seven leaflets per leaf.

J. sambac (Arabian jasmine) is an evergreen rambler with tight clusters of three or more fragrant white flowers that acquire hints of pink and purple as they age. The species can grow up to 30' tall in the right conditions. **'Grand Duke of Tuscany'** is a slower growing cultivar with leaves arranged in sets of three and solitary double flowers in creamy pale yellow. The flowers are also quite large in comparison. **'Maid of Orleans'** is exceptionally fragrant, producing single, crisp white, flattish flowers.

J. nudiflorum used as a screen (above); *J. x stephanense* grown around a post (below)

Harvest and Processing

The flowers can be picked fresh or dried throughout the blooming cycle and used for their scent. Store them in airtight containers to preserve their perfume for as long as possible.

Uses

Both fresh and dried flowers can be used in sachets, potpourri, herbal pillows and scented wreaths. The flowers can also be steeped in warmed water or aromatherapy baths to stimulate the senses. They are even said to act as an aphrodisiac. The flowers can also be added to hand-made toiletries and bath products, including soaps, hair and facial rinses, lotions and bath bombs.

Jasmine has been and is used medicinally, but it should be used only under the close supervision of a professional medical practitioner. Never take it internally on your own.

Basic rules to follow when growing jasmine: choose a cool location in winter; place it outdoors in summer; and provide plenty of light and support.

Kaffir Lime

Citrus

Kaffir lime may conjure up visions of Asian cuisine, which makes more use of the leaves than the fruit. You can find Kaffir lime leaves in most Asian markets and some supermarkets, but growing this plant at home will provide you with fresh leaves year round, whether it's outdoors for the summer or indoors for the winter. Kaffir lime provides the tangy, citrus flavor and perfume common in many Thai soups and salads, stir-fries and curries, and if you've ever tried a dish containing this herb, you may just find yourself growing this at home to experiment.

Fresh chopped leaves (left) and dried leaves (right)

Features

Parts used: leaves, fruit
Hardiness: tropical, zone 9, grown as an annual or container plant

Growing

As with most other citrus plants, kaffir lime prefers to grow in **full to partial sun**. The soil or potting mix should be **well drained, moist, organically rich** and **soil based**. Pruning may be necessary to keep it dense and to encourage it to produce more leaves.

Tips

Grow kaffir lime in a container so you can move it outdoors during the summer. Plant it as a specimen and keep it in a loose, natural or topiary form. Move it back indoors long before the sign of frost in the fall.

Recommended

C. hystrix produces leathery, shiny leaves in a teardrop shape resembling wings or an hourglass. Fragrant, white flowers emerge from woody stems during the longest days of summer. In the right conditions, this species can grow up to 6', but is better kept at 4–5' tall or shorter, so you can move it more easily. It bears fragrant white blossoms and knobby-skinned, bright green fruits approximately 4" wide, with a few thorns along the stems.

Harvesting and Processing

The leaves can be harvested all year long. Use them fresh, dried or frozen. To freeze, place a group of leaves into two layers of tin foil. Dry leaves by placing them onto screens out of direct light. Once dry, store them in airtight containers. The fruit rind can also be dried for later use just as you would the leaves or freeze whole fruits in freezer bags and take out only to grate the rind.

Uses

Kaffir lime leaves are to Southeast Asian cuisine what bay leaves are to Mediterranean cooking. Shredded finely and added to stews and sauces, the leaves impart a subtle citrus flavor. For simmering in soups or curries, use the whole leaves and remove before serving.

Kaffir lime rind and juice are also used to flavor soups and curry pastes, as well as cold drinks. The zest is widely used in Creole cooking.

Lavender

Lavandula

All parts of the lavender plant are aromatic and useful in a variety of ways.
Lavender has been used medicinally for centuries for the treatment of stomach
complaints and fainting, even though herbalists were suspicious of its properties
because of the essential oil's "fierce and piercing quality." Today herbalists
recognize its value and use it to treat insomnia, anxiety, depression, indigestion
and a variety of skin problems. Crafters have a special appreciation for lavender
because of its versatility and heavenly aroma, and it has culinary uses in all things
sweet. Someone was even creative
enough to discover its repellent
properties as a natural herbicide.
Grow lavender purely for its
beauty and dreamy scent.

Lavender and roses make fragrant companions

Features

Parts used: flowers, leaves
Hardiness: zones 4–9

Growing

Lavender grow best in **full sun**. The soil should be **average to fertile, alkaline** and **well drained**. In colder areas, lavenders should be covered with mulch and a good layer of snow. The key to winter survival is good drainage—often, winterkill results from wet "feet," not from cold. Lavender never needs supplemental watering and will do best on rainfall alone unless there is an extended drought.

Both 'Hidcote' and 'Munstead' lavender are named after English estate gardens.

Tips

Lavenders are wonderful edging plants. Good companions for these deer-resistant plants include other drought-tolerant specimens such as pinks, thyme, lamb's ears and sedum. A herbal garden wouldn't be complete without lavender. Place containers filled with lavender nearby, so you can enjoy its fragrance.

Recommended

L. angustifolia (English lavender) is an aromatic, bushy perennial. From mid-summer to fall, it bears spikes of small flowers in varied shades of violet blue that stand above fragrant, silvery green foliage. **'Hidcote'** is also compact with deep purple flowers and silvery grey leaves (Zones 4–8). **'Hidcote Pink'** has pink flowers and **'Munstead'** produces bluish purple flowers earlier than most in a compact form (Zones 4–9). **'Nana Alba'** is very compact with pure white flowers (Zones 5–8) and **'Rosea'** ('Jean Davis') is a compact selection with pale pink flowers (Zones 5–8). **'Royal Purple'** produces dark blue-purple flowers (Zones 5–9).

L. dentata (French lavender, fringed lavender) is a sub-shrub that grows 36" tall and 5' wide. It produces scalloped, needle-like leaves and purple-blue flowers (Zones 8–9).

Lavender blooms emerging (above); lavender topiary (below)

Lavender is a fine companion plant to thyme and a good influence on vegetables, making them tastier and healthier.

L. 'Goodwin Creek Grey' bears silvery grey, toothed foliage and deep purple-blue flowers (Zones 7–9).

L. x *intermedia* (lavandin) is a rounded shrub with branching stems bearing grey-green, spoon-shaped leaves. Light blue to purple flower spikes emerge in summer. This hybrid will reach 22–36" in height and spread. **'Alba'** produces white flowers and grey leaves. **'Dutch'** has dark purple flowers. **'Fred Boutin'** is a low-growing selection with silvery, woolly foliage and violet flowers. **'Grosso'** has a very strong scent with violet flowers. **'Provence'** produces dark purple flowers (Zones 5–9).

L. *multifida* 'Spanish Eyes' is an annual with fern-like, green foliage and bright blue-lavender flowers. It grows 24" tall and wide (Zone 9).

L. *stoechas* (Italian lavender, Spanish lavender) is a compact and bushy plant bearing dark purple flowers and linear, green leaves. It grows 24" tall and wide (Zones 8–9). **'Kew Red'** bears dark magenta red flowers topped with pale pink bracts (Zones 7–9). **'Otto Quast'** produces royal

Lavender-scented dream pillow (above); lavender-scented bath salts (below)

purple flowers and grey-blue fragrant foliage. **Subsp.** *pedunculata* (Spanish long lavender) produces large, magenta flowers and grows almost 36" tall (Zones 8–9). **'Purple Ribbon'** produces large, purple flowers with wing-like bracts (Zones 7–9).

Harvesting and Processing

Pick lavender just before the last flowers on the stalks open fully. The oil content in the blossoms is the most potent at this stage. Cut stems on a dry day, before the heat of the sun draws out the oils. Hang the bunches in a dry, airy location. Drying racks are ideal for this purpose. Once dry, either strip the flowers from the stems and store in airtight containers, or leave stems intact for arrangements. Fresh, pliable stems can be braided, twisted and knotted into lavender rope.

Uses

Use lavender to decorate sweet treats or add them to the ingredients for a unique flavor. Lavender shortbread for example, is very tasty.

The scent of lavender calms frayed nerves when added to a warm bath. Lavender oil when massaged into rheumatic joints eases discomfort.

Crafters use lavender and its essence to scent various bath products and fragrances. Whole stems and flowers can be braided into garlands or used to fill sachets. The oil can be added to distilled water to make skin fresheners, lip balm, massage oil, foot soaks and room fresheners.

Lemon Balm

Melissa

This lemon-scented and -flavored herb is indispensable to those who love a touch of lemon in most dishes. This herb is incredibly easy to grow, regardless of what zone you live in or your level of gardening expertise. Lemon scented and flavored herbs are also very versatile for cooking, crafts and cosmetics, as well as natural medicines. Lemon balm is a fine companion plant to other herbs and vegetables, which seem to grow bigger and have better flavor and aroma when lemon balm is planted close by. Some even say that growing lemon balm in pastures where cows graze increases their milk production. If you're without a herd of cows in your backyard, you'll still find lemon balm to be one of the most important herbs in your garden.

Lemon balm grown in a raised bed

Features
Other names: balm
Parts used: leaves
Hardiness: zones 3–7

Growing
Lemon balm prefers to grow in **full sun** but will grow quite successfully in locations with dappled shade. The soil should be **moist, fertile** and **well drained** but it can tolerate poor, dry soils. *M.* 'All Gold' requires some shade to prevent the foliage scorching. This cultivar may also need a little winter protection in zones colder than 4.

Taking cuttings for use will encourage dense and vigorous growth. It's best to remove the flowers as they emerge.

Tips
Lemon balm is a self-seeder and may spread throughout your garden—it is related to mint which has a similar habit. Lemon balm is not as invasive, however. Herb gardens are often the preferred location for this useful perennial, but it also works well as

A particular type of honey, prized since the 16th century, is the result of beehives located near patches of lemon balm.

Lemon balm adds flavor to cold drinks.

Lemon balm in a mixed container with viola and pineapple mint

a fragrant filler in containers, mixed beds and borders. Lemon balm is a well known bee and butterfly plant and will attract other pollinating insects.

Recommended

M. officinalis is a bushy, densely growing perennial with roughly textured, hairy leaves that are fragrant and flavorful when bruised or crushed. Flowers are produced but are considered inconspicuous. It grows 24" tall and wide. **'All Gold'** has yellow foliage and **'Aurea'** produces gold and green mottled leaves in a variegated form. **'Citronella'** is the most fragrant cultivar available. It has double the oil content compared to other selections and has a slightly

more compact form. **'Lemonella'** is very similar to the former cultivar in aroma and overall mature size. **'Lime'** produces an aroma more reminiscent of lime than oranges but the overall look is the same. **'Quedlingburger'** is a taller cultivar with good oil content in its foliage.

Harvesting and Processing

Pick the leaves throughout the growing season. Fresh leaves definitely offer the strongest flavor and it's best to harvest the leaves before the flowers open, when the essential oils in the leaves are at their most potent. At the end of the season, before hard frost, cut the entire plant down at soil level. Spread the stems and leaves out onto a screen to dry. Once they are

Lemon balm is used to scent lotions and potpourri.

dry, strip the leaves from the stems and store in airtight containers. Fresh leaves can also be stored year round for later use when chopped finely and added to ice cube trays with a little water.

Uses

Use the leaves fresh or dried for teas, both hot and cold. Blend one or more of the following herbs with lemon balm to find your favorite combination: anise seeds, peppermint, chamomile, beebalm, basil, cardamon pods, fennel seeds and rose hips. All of these complement the citrus flavor of lemon balm.

Infused in boiling water, the leaves can be used to make a rinse for oily hair, a skin freshener and moisturizer, or simply to scent bath water. The dried leaves can be added to potpourri, herbal pillows and sachets.

There are many culinary uses for lemon balm, mainly in foods that require no cooking because the flavor is lost when the leaves are heated. Fresh leaves are a lemony treat when added to cool drinks, salads or crystallized for decorating desserts. Their flavor is also a nice addition to marmalades and jams, fish dishes and soups. It can be combined with other strong-flavored herbs as a seasoning for poultry dishes, lamb, port and stewed fruit.

Lemon is an important and popular scent in aromatherapy. It is said to relieve depression, stress, tension and headaches, and to sharpen memory.

Lemongrass
Cymbopogon

Just the thought of lemongrass makes our mouths water, reminding us of the yummy things that we love about this herb. Asian cuisines, more specifically Thai, Chinese and Vietnamese, all use this fresh, revitalizing and tasty plant, and it is worthy of more kitchen experimentation. Crafters are also fond of this plant. Its essence is good for the skin, giving it a luminous glow; so try adding a little to your bath water. Medicinally, lemongrass is a tonic for the kidneys, and can sooth a fever. It is also just refreshing on a hot summer day.

Features
Other names: Indian lemon grass
Parts used: leaves, tender shoots
Hardiness: tender perennial grown in containers, or as an annual

Growing
Lemongrass prefers to be grown in **hot** and **sunny** locations in **very well drained, sandy, moist soil**. Be sure to water thoroughly and more frequently during dry, hot spells. Divide in spring.

As a companion plant, this influential herb will improve the flavor and aroma of other herbs and vegetables in the garden.

Tips

This grassy-looking plant is perfectly suited to warm, if not hot, sunny locations in your garden. Lemongrass tolerates dry areas as well. It can be integrated into your mixed flower-beds as a foliar accent or added to a herb garden purely for practical purposes. It can also be grown in containers, allowing you to bring it indoors in winter.

Recommended

C. citratus (West Indian lemongrass) is a stocky, clump-forming grass with hollow, cane-like stems. Long, narrow, arching leaves emerge from the base of the stems, aromatic and bluish green in color. This species grows 36" or more in height and 12–24" in spread.

Harvesting and Processing

Cut the leaves almost to the base in the fall, when the clump is full and dense. Dry the stems by hanging bunches in a cool, dry location or spread them out on drying racks or screens. Once dry, cut to fit into air-tight containers. The swollen stems can be used whole, cut into slices or bruised to release their lemony oils.

Uses

Lemongrass can be used whenever a lemon flavor is desired. Use the tips of the leaves, the tender shoots and whole leaves in the cooking process and discarded just before serving. Add the chopped, tender leaves to steaming fish or chichken, into a simmering soup or to hot water for

Dried lemongrass and lemon oil

a refreshing tea. Add bruised stems to broths, stews and curries, and remove before serving. To release the oils from the swollen base of the stems, bruise the outer layers with the back of a knife.

The essential oil is used in bath products, handmade soaps and lotions, fragrances, sachets, potpourri and room fresheners. Medicinally, lemongrass has antiseptic properties and is used externally to treat rheumatic aches and pains, and internally for indigestion and upset tummies.

Mature lemongrass plants

Lemon Verbena

Aloysia

Lemon verbena is one of the most popular lemon-scented herbs and is also one of the most versatile. Its fresh leaves can be used to flavor oils and vinegars, drinks, desserts, stuffings and fragrant sachets for year-round enjoyment. After a strenuous day in the garden or at the gym, drop a bunch of fresh lemon verbena leaves into a hot bath and the lemony fragrance will subtly scent your skin and reinvigorate your tired muscles and spirit. The leaves have medicinal properties as well. If you're an insomniac, try lemon verbena tea as a sedative. It will also help to relieve or reduce fevers and indigestion. On a blisteringly hot summer day, it's the quintessential garnish on a cool, fruity drink.

Features
Parts used: leaves, flowers
Hardiness: zones 9–11; tender
shrub grown in containers,
or as an annual

Growing

Lemon verbena prefers a **sunny** location. The soil should be **light, well drained** and **moderately fertile**. It is best grown from starter plants rather than from seed. Wait to plant out at least one to two weeks after the last spring frost. Plants may overwinter when planted in a location with good drainage shelter. This herb has a bit of a leggy growth habit, but you can let plants grow as they will, or you can prune or train them into standard or topiary forms.

Tips

Grow lemon verbena in a container in colder regions so it can be brought inside for the winter. Plant it with other herbs in a strawberry pot for interest, or alone in a decorative container. Give it lots of room when planted with other plants. It also grows well in the garden.

Recommended

A. triphylla produces pale green, narrow leaves that smell strongly of lemon. Tiny, white flowers tinged with pale purple emerge in early summer. It grows 3–4" tall and 12–36" wide.

Harvesting and Processing

Fresh mature leaves are most flavorful. Pinch the newest leaves often, to encourage new, dense and bushy growth. Pick the leaves before the flowers emerge or open. Flowers may not even form in a short season, but if they do, harvest for use. Harvest several bunches of leafy stems, strip the leaves and chop finely, mix with water and freeze in ice cube trays for use over the winter. Dry the leaves and flowers by hanging them in

Lemon verbena tea

bunches in a cool, airy location, and store in airtight containers once dry.

Use

Use the leaves fresh alone or combined with other herbs for tea. A pinch of dried leaves can be added to stuffing, sauces or ice cream and desserts.

Crafters love this herb because it retains its strong lemon scent for years. Add it to sachets and dream pillows. A mixture of chamomile flowers, a crushed cinnamon stick, marigold petals, the dried peel of one lemon and lemon verbena leaves, with a hint of the essential oil is ideal for potpourri. Because it has insecticidal properties lemon balm wards off moths and other insects when used in sach closets, wardrobes and dresse the essential oil to scent ba or homemade air fresher

Licorice

Glycyrrhiza

Licorice is one of those herbs, or flavors more specifically, that people either love or hate. Aside from flavoring tasty treats, licorice has abundant medicinal and cosmetic uses. If you want to try something new, licorice may be just the thing because of its rarity in our gardens and pantries.

Features
Parts used: root
Hardiness: zones 5–8

Growing
Licorice requires **full sun** but will tolerate partial sun. The soil should be **deep, moist** and **rich with organic matter**. It's best to begin with starter plants, at least one or more years old. If only seed is available, then be patient because germination is slow. Start the seed early, indoors so you can plant the seedlings into a container in summer. When growing it

in the ground, dedicate a space in the garden for licorice because it spreads vigorously underground each year, sending up delicate foliage from new roots.

Tips

Plant the tender licorices in a container so you can bring them indoors for the winter; plants must grow 3 to 4 years before the roots can be harvested. A hot and sunny herb bed or south-facing deck, balcony or patio are ideal locations to grow this herb.

Recommended

G. echinata (Russian licorice) is the hardiest of the three species recommended here. It produces pale blue violet blossoms followed by pods covered with spines. This well-branched plant is dense and bushy, producing a myriad of lush, bright green leaves, similar to *G. glabra*. It produces violet flowers and seedpods that grows to 4–5' heights and 3–4' spreads (Zone 5).

G. glabra (licorice, sweet wood) is the most popular of the group, and can grow up to 4' in height with a significant yellow and fibrous taproot. The sticky leaves are made up of leaflets, 9–17 per leaf. It bears short spikes of violet or white, pealike flowers followed by decorative brown seed pods (Zone 7).

G. uralensis (Chinese licorice, sweet grass, sweet herb) is the most commonly used species for medicinal purposes, particularly Chinese medicine. It is also the least hardy of the bunch. It grows up to 4' tall and is less dense and bushy than its counterparts. Small clusters of small lilac flowers are followed by interesting reddish, bristly pods (Zone 6).

G. glabra

Harvesting and Processing

Dig the roots up after the plant is 3 to 4 years old. Once the roots are dug up, separate them from the stems and dry them. Once dried, grind the roots or leave them whole. Licorice can become toxic if you ingest too much, so make sure to research how much to take and when.

Uses

The roots are usually dried and powdered for use as a sweetener (it is 50 times sweeter than sugar) or to flavor candy and liquor. Licorice extract has also been used to flavor beer and soft drinks.

Crafters use licorice essence in handmade soaps, lotions and bath products.

Medicinally, licorice can be used for treating coughs, wheezing and shortness of breath. It's often added to cough medicines and lozenges. It can be used as a gentle laxative, or to calm an upset stomach. Licorice is also prescribed by homeopathic doctors for balancing blood sugar levels. Use it only in consultation with a qualified practitioner.

Licorice should not be given to pregnant women or to people with high blood pressure or kidney disease because it can raise blood pressure.

Lovage

Levisticum

Lovage is also known as love parsley, but it tastes more like celery with a peppery bite. It is native to parts of the Mediterranean and found its way to North America generations ago. It is one of the lesser known herbs today, but it deserves a comeback. It was once used frequently both for culinary and medicinal purposes. Lovage even has cosmetic uses and is a fine companion to root vegetables, having "an enlivening effect" on their flavor and overall appeal.

Features
Other names: love parsley, sea parsley
Parts used: leaves, roots, stems, seeds
Hardiness: zones 3–9

Growing

Lovage prefers **full sun to partial shade**. The soil should be **deep, rich** and **moist**. It is easiest to start with young plants, but sowing seed is an alternative. Be sure to start the seed early in spring after last frost. Divide established plants in spring.

Tips

Lovage is the perfect addition to the herb or kitchen garden. It is attractive enough to with flowering perennials in a mixed border as well. You can grow lovage in decorative containers, but keep it well clipped so it doesn't overwhelm the pot.

Recommended

L. officinale produces pale green, ornate leaflets in groups of three. It can grow quite tall in a short season, bearing upright stalks clothed in foliage. Large, flat heads of small flowers form clusters high above the foliage in summer in white and yellow. It grows 3–4' tall and 24–36" wide.

Harvesting and Processing

Use the leaves either fresh or dried throughout the season, but to store them for winter use, chop them up, add water and add to ice cube trays. To dry the leaves, spread them out onto screens or hang bunches of leafy stems on drying racks. Once dry, store in airtight containers. Use stems fresh; harvest roots and seeds at the end of the season and dry for later use as you would leaves. Harvest the seeds when they have begun to turn brown and pick them on a dry day. Dig up the roots after the second or third season. The leaves are somewhat bitter

Flowering lovage

after the plant has flowered. If this is undesirable, remove the flowers as they emerge.

Uses

Lovage has many culinary uses. The leaves and shoots can be cooked and eaten as vegetables, while the seeds can be added to soups, stews and baked goods. Chopped leaves are a delicious addition to soups and casseroles. Leafy stems can be blanched and eaten, but stay away from the central flower stems, which are inedible. The leaves are also the perfect flavoring for fish, meat and vegetable dishes.

Medicinally, lovage was used to treat indigestion and is still prescribed by herbalists today, in tea form to promote digestion and rheumatism.

The perfume industry has used the essence of lovage in fragrances.

Marigold
Tagetes

It's safe to say that almost everyone loves marigolds—it's hard not to. It may sound a little corny, but bright, sunny flowers are pretty hard to hate. Aside from their sunny disposition, marigolds have a lot to offer. Reminiscent of spicy tarragon, marigolds are a tasty treat for the health conscious because of their medicinal benefits. Tuck them into your containers, flowerbeds, window boxes and vegetable gardens.

Features
Parts used: flowers, leaves of *T. lucida*
Hardiness: annual

Growing
Marigolds grow best in **full sun**. The soil should be of **average fertility** and **well drained**. These plants are drought tolerant and hold up well in windy, rainy weather. Remove spent blooms to encourage more flowers and to keep plants tidy. Start seed indoors in spring or earlier, or plant seedlings once soil has warmed.

Tips

Mass planted or mixed with other plants, marigolds make a vibrant addition to beds, borders and container gardens. These plants will thrive in the hottest, driest parts of your garden.

Recommended

T. lucida (Mexican tarragon, Mexican marigold, sweet mace, sweet marigold) is a woody-based perennial with anise-scented, toothed leaves and sweetly scented yellow flowers. It grows 12–30" tall and 18" wide. This species is an absolute must for Mexican cooking. The flowers taste like tarragon.

T. tenuifolia (*T. signata*, signet marigold, rock garden marigold) is an upright annual that produces branchy stems with narrow, lance-shaped leaves, with deeply toothed edges. Single flowers bearing yellow or orange petals are borne throughout summer. The species grows 12–16" tall and 12–18" wide. Hybrids are available, including the **Pumila Series**, a dwarf group bearing finely fringed leaves and lemony scented flowers. **Gem Hybrids** also have a dwarf habit and bear single flowers in shades of orange and yellow. This includes '**Lemon Gem**' and '**Orange Gem**,' both of which are bright, colorful and pleasantly citrus flavored.

Other marigold species, hybrids and cultivars can be used for culinary purposes, but because they taste bitter, they are used more as garnishes.

Harvesting and Processing

Use marigold flowers fresh. They tend to lose their flavor and color

Marigold salad

when dried, and they don't freeze well. Collect a few flowers just before you need them, to preserve the rich color and aroma. Harvest the foliage anytime; the youngest leaves are the best.

Mid-morning is the best time to harvest, before the temperature rises and after the dew evaporates. Once the flowers are open, clip them from the stem. Remove the outer petals and bitter centers.

Uses

The species *T. lucida* is used as a culinary or tea herb in some Latin American countries, and its petals add a piquant note to a salad. The petals can also be sprinkled on casseroles, soups and meat and fish dishes. Its flowers are an ideal substitute for tarragon.

Mint

Mentha

Mint. Well surely this is an easy one? Mint is a simple and effective herb on so many levels. It's incredibly easy to grow, and will take on a life of its own, spreading across your entire yard if you let it. The selections are endless, including ginger-flavored and lemony mint, and every one is useful in a wide variety of dishes. Mint also has many medicinal benefits, and crafters are well aware of the versatility of this herb. Just think of the many things you know right off the top of your head that are mint-flavored or scented. The possibilities are simply endless.

A bundle of herbs including mint makes a nice addition to a hot bath.

Features
Parts used: leaves
Hardiness: zones 3–8

Growing
Mint grows well in **full sun** and **partial shade**. The soil should be **average to fertile, humus-rich** and **moist**. These plants spread vigorously by rhizomes and may need a barrier in the soil to restrict their spread.

Tips
Mint is a good groundcover for damp spots. It grows well along ditches that may be only periodically wet. It also can be used in beds and borders, but may overwhelm less vigorous plants. To contain mint's aggressive growth habit, plant this herb in containers. The pots can either be overwintered outdoors, depending on the region you live in, or brought indoors and placed near a windowsill for year-round use.

The flowers attract bees, butterflies and other pollinators to the garden.

To contain your mint to a small patch in the garden, plant it in a large plastic bucket with the bottom cut out. Bury the bucket in the location you desire, with the top extending approximately 3" above ground. This will contain it to the bucket, forcing it to stay put.

Recommended
There are many species, hybrids and cultivars of mint. The following are only a few of the great selections available.

M. **x gracilis** (gingermint, redmint) is a spicy selection with a flavor reminiscent of ginger. **'Variegata'** produces green leaves with yellow variegations. Spearmint (*M. spicata*), peppermint (*M.* x *piperita*) and orange mint (*M.* x *piperata citrata*) are three of the

To control mint's vigorous growth, grow it in pots.

most commonly grown culinary varieties. There are also more decorative varieties with variegated or curly leaves as well as varieties with unusual, fruit-scented leaves.

M. suaveolens (applemint, woolly mint) produces hairy leaves suitable for candying and considered to be superior in flavor. **'Berries and Cream'**, a Westerfield mint, is sweet and fruity, and **'Margarita'** produces bold, lime-scented foliage. **'Pink Candypops'** was bred with esthetics in mind, producing large pink flower puffs in summer. **'Sweet Pear'**, another of the many Westerfield-bred mints, smells and tastes of pear. **'Variegata'** produces leaves touched with white and cream markings.

Blending a little chopped mint, diluted vinegar and sugar will result in a delicious mint sauce suitable for lamb dishes.

Harvesting and Processing

As with many other herbs, mint is most flavorful and aromatic when used fresh and harvested before it goes to flower. Sometimes there just isn't the opportunity to use it fresh, however. Pinch off leaves throughout the growing season for everyday use. Once the season is coming to an end, or your mint patch is allowing you to keep pace, harvest bunches of stems to freeze and dry. For year-round, fresh mint, simply chop mint leaves, and add them to a little water in ice cube trays. Dried mint, if stored in airtight containers, retains its flavor and scent very well. Either hang tied bunches on drying racks or spread them out onto screens until completely dry. Strip the leaves from the stems and store in airtight containers. A few leafy stems can also be wrapped in foil or stored in an airtight bag in the freezer for immediate use; they will keep for a few weeks.

Uses

It's not difficult to find a zillion ways to use this herb. A few sprigs of fresh mint added to a pitcher of iced tea gives it an added zip. Chopped leaves mixed into a stick of butter, after a brief period in the refrigerator and cut into squares, results in a tasty treat on crackers or toast. Spearmint butter is the perfect complement to lamb. Different types of mint can be mixed together to switch things up a little. Apple mint and spearmint are the perfect combination for mint sauce. Every type of mint works well with fresh fruit, tea and cool drinks such as lemonade. Try new dishes with mint; sprinkle chopped leaves on new potatoes or tomatoes, egg dishes, ice cream or mix them into cream cheese. Spearmint is a popular herb in Mediterranean and Middle Eastern cuisine. It lends a distinct flavor to meat and vegetable dishes. It's also commonly used in sauces, soups and salads. My personal favorite is mint tea, regardless of whether it is spearmint, peppermint or orange mint. Mint tea is a soothing, refreshing drink that can be enjoyed at any time of day and is said to relieve indigestion, promote sound sleep and helps to ward off colds in the winter, if taken regularly.

Mint scented and flavored products are abundant and for good reason. Spearmint is often used in toothpaste because it helps with bad breath, whitens teeth and conditions the gums. Mint is commonly used to scent a variety of handmade bath products, lotions and room fresheners. The leaves are a refreshing addition to potpourri and sleep pillows. A generous bunch of mint can be dropped into a hot bath as a restorative treat.

Minty Ice tea (above); mint potpourri (below)

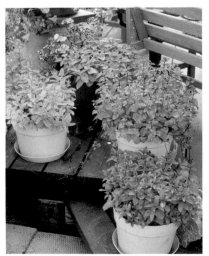

Potted mint varieties

Mountain Mint

Pycnanthemum

Mountain mint may smell and taste like mint, but it is not a "true" mint, even though it is part of the same family, *Lamiaceae.* This aromatic herb can be used in cooking, but it can also be used medicinally to remedy stomach upsets, sinus headaches and colds. With a variety of species to choose from, mountain mint is simply a beautiful, fragrant plant perfectly suited to any garden in the Midwest.

Features
Other names: Virginia mountain mint, wild basil, prairie hyssop
Parts used: whole plant, leaves, flowers, buds
Hardiness: zones 5–10

Growing
Mountain mint prefers to grow in **full sun to partial shade**. The soil should be **rich** and **well drained**. Directly sow seed in spring or fall, or propagate by division when dormant.

Tips
Mountain mint is an ideal specimen for the vegetable or herb garden. Planted in clumps, mountain mint will draw attention to its white- and lilac-colored flowers. Plant this herb near a pathway, whether in a bed, a border or a container, so you can smell its heavenly scent as you walk by.

Recommended
P. virginianum (mountain mint) is a perennial with pointed leaves on tall stems that produce a peppery but minty flavor. White- to lilac-colored flowers are borne at the tips of the stems in dense, flat-topped heads in late summer. This species grows 28–36" tall and 8–24" wide.

   P. incanum (gray mountain mint) has stems, leaves and flowerbuds that are covered in a soft, silvery hairs. This species can grow 4–6' tall.

Harvesting and Processing
All parts of the plant can be collected for fresh use as the flowering cycle begins. The flowers and buds can also be dried after harvest for use in infusions. The leafy stems can be laid out on screens to dry, hung on drying racks or from the rafters of a cool, dark room with adequate air circulation.

Mountain mint flowers in late summer

Uses
The flowering tops and buds are a pleasant mint-like addition to savory dishes, particularly meat dishes. Fresh and dried flowers can be used for tea. Fresh flowers can also be sprinkled sparingly into salads.

   The oils in the leaves act as a natural insecticide when rubbed on clothes while outdoors.

   Crafters will love this herb, as the dried stems are ideal for dried arrangements, sachets, potpourri and dream pillows.

Pregnant women or women who may think they are pregnant should not consume any species or any part of *Pycnanthemum*.

Nasturtium

Tropaeolum

Nasturtiums are a mainstay annual in my garden and in my kitchen. I use the flowers and leaves as garnishes, in salads and as pizza toppings. But beware of hiding insects such as earwigs and aphids—clean the flowers and leaves well. This beauty is incredibly easy to grow and will reward you with an abundance of warmly colored flowers that are not only pretty to look at, but also pleasing to the palate.

Features

Other names: Indian cress, garden nasturtium
Parts used: flowers, leaves, seeds
Hardiness: annual

Growing

Nasturtiums prefer **full sun** but tolerate some shade. The soil should be of **average to poor fertility, light, moist** and **well drained**. Too rich a soil or too much nitrogen fertilizer will result in lots of leaves and very few flowers. Let the soil drain completely between waterings. If you start nasturtium seeds indoors, sow them in individual peat pots to avoid disturbing the roots during transplanting.

Tips

Nasturtiums are used in beds, borders, containers and hanging baskets, and on sloped banks and other poor locations. The climbing varieties are grown up trellises or over rock walls or places that need concealing.

If you find aphids on the plants, they will likely congregate near the growing tips. Cut the infested parts off and drop them in a bucket of soapy water.

Recommended

T. majus has a trailing habit. It has been greatly improved by hybridizing. The foliage of the older varieties tended to hide the flowers, but new varieties hold their flowers (available in a great selection of colors) above the foliage. There are also some new and interesting cultivars with variegated foliage and compact, attractive, mound-forming habits. **Alaska Series** plants have white-marbled foliage. **Jewel Series** plants are compact, growing 12" tall and wide, with double flowers in a mix of deep orange, red or gold. **'Peach Melba'** forms a 12" mound. The flowers are pale yellow with a bright orange-red splash at the base of each petal. **'Whirlybird'** is a

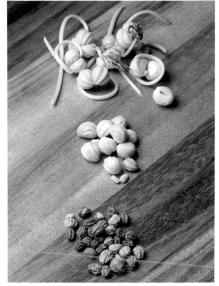

Nasturtium seeds, fresh (top) and dried (bottom)

compact, bushy plant. The single or double flowers in shades of red, pink, yellow or orange do not have spurs.

Harvesting and Processing

Pick the flowers and leaves throughout the growing season for fresh use. The seeds can either be harvested from the plant in the fall before they lose their green color, or seed can be purchased from the garden center. Make sure to buy seed that has NOT been treated with anything, including fungicides.

Uses

Eat the leaves and flowers fresh in sandwiches, salads or blended into dips. They should never be eaten cooked, frozen or dried. Blend them into cottage cheese for a peppery flavor or use as a garnish. Pickle the seeds and eat them as you would capers. Toss them into salads for a little bit of peppery bite.

Use nasturtium sparingly. No more than $1/2$ oz should be consumed at one time, or 1oz daily.

Onion

Allium

Onions are thought of as vegetables and herbs, depending on the species, where you live and how you use them. Either way, onions are a staple in everyday cooking, offering a flavor that is unique compared to any other herb. Onions are quite possibly one of the oldest used herbs, thought to go back to a time before historians, leaving us uncertain of their origins. That being said, there are quite a few onions to choose from and rightly so. Each type of onion has a particular use. They're all easy to grow however and require little in the way of maintenance.

Features

Parts used: swollen bulb or root, fresh juice, (whole plant including leaves— Welsh onion only)
Hardiness: zones 4–9

Onions are thought to ward off colds and induce sleep as well cure indigestion. Herbalists also prescribe fresh onion juice to treat coughs, colds, bronchitis, laryngitis and gastroenteritis.

Growing

Onions grow well in locations with **full sun**. Onions prefer soil that is **well drained** and **fertile**. Seed for Welsh onions can be sown directly into the soil in spring after the risk of frost has passed. Mulch with well-rotted manure in the fall. Divide clumps every few years in spring.

Flowering *A. fistulosum* in a mixed bed of annuals and perennials

Bulbs sets for *A. cepa* should be planted in clusters approximately 12–18" apart. Don't expect too much in the first year. Mulch with a well-rotted manure in the fall, and the following year you should harvest a mass of small onions. Bend over the tops of the stems in late summer to speed up the ripening process. Dry the bulbs before storing.

Tips

Onions are usually relegated to the vegetable garden but they are also a beautiful addition to the herb garden. They can also be grown in containers for sunny locations outdoors.

Recommended

A. cepa (onion) is a biennial that produces a thick stem made up of layered, hollow leaves that emerge from a single 4" wide bulb at the base of the stem. **Proliferum Group**, (var. proliferum, tree onion, Egyptian onion) is a hardy perennial plant that can produce foliage 3–5' in height. It bears small, greenish-white flowers in early summer at the tips of the leaves or stems, followed by bulbs or bulbils. Bulbs are also produced in the soil. The bulbils at the ends of the stems produce a small root system, capable of reproducing another plant if separated from the mother plant. **'Ailsa Craig'** has straw-colored skin,

Onions are a staple in many cuisines.

a mild flavor and a rounded bulb. **'Noordhollandse Bloedrode'** ('North Holland Blood Red') also has a milder flavored bulb with deep red skin and pink flesh. **'Sweet Sandwich'** is a large cultivar with brown-skinned bulbs that become very sweet and mild after two months in storage.

A. fistulosum (Welsh onion, Japanese leek, scallion, spring onion) is an evergreen perennial or biennial that produces 24–36" tall foliage and cylindrical bulbs. In the second year of growth, it bears greenish yellow flowers in early summer. The leaves are narrow, deep green and hollow in the center. **'White Lisbon'** is a white-skinned cultivar with a milder flavor than the species and a much larger mature bulb. It grows 8–12" tall.

Harvesting and Processing

Welsh onions can be picked at any time throughout the growing season. The leaves are edible, too, and are best eaten fresh. Since they do not dry well, it's best to chop them finely,

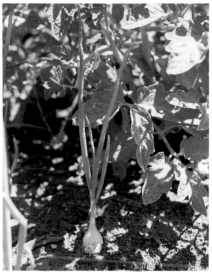

Onion bulb forming (above);
A. cepa red and white onions (below)

add a little water and fill an ice cube tray for later use. Tree onions can be picked from the stems and stored in a cool place with adequate air circulation.

Uses

Welsh onions are useful both fresh and cooked in just about any dish that requires onions, especially in Chinese cuisine. They are tasty in stir-fries, salads, sandwiches and in any dish that uses chives.

The bulbils from tree onions can be pickled, used raw in salads for a little kick, or cooked whole in casseroles, stews and soups. Just about any meat, fish or vegetable dish will benefit from the addition of this onion.

Medicinally, the Welsh onion has decongestant and antibacterial properties, similar to garlic. Any species from the *Allium* genus is useful in

lowering blood pressure and blood cholesterol. Onions are also helpful in preventing blood clotting, which can prevent circulatory diseases.

It was once thought that hanging a bunch of onions outside the door would ward off the plague.

Orach

Atriplex

What is orach? Well, let me introduce you to this interesting, tasty plant. Orach has had a number of uses in herbal medicine over the centuries, but today it is used more for cooking. Orach can be grown as a vegetable, using the leaves as you would spinach. Because of its tender nature, you may want to grow it indoors year-round; just make sure its soil is moist and its location is bright and sunny, to prevent stretching. Supplementing the sunlight with a grow light will keep plants strong and stocky through the winter. When the leaves and stems become too long and tough, clip them off at soil level for use in dried or fresh flower arrangements for something a little different.

Features

Other names: French spinach
Parts used: leaves
Hardiness: annual

Growing

Orach prefers to grow in **full to partial sun**. The red-leaved cultivar benefits from partial shade. The soil should be **moist and well drained**. Larger leaves will be produced when the herb is grown in organically rich soil. It is best to sow seed in late spring after the risk has passed. Plant seedlings or small starter plants after last frost as well. Orach is very vigorous. Deadhead regularly and water during dry periods to prevent bolting.

Tips

Orach can be grown strictly as an ornamental or one with practical uses in mixed beds and borders. Red orach in particular is stunning when mixed with yellow-leaved plants or those with flowers borne in fiery colors. Orach will grow quite successfully in containers. To maintain its height, pinch out the tips from time to time to encourage bushier growth without allowing it to outgrow its pot. Be careful not to water this plant during the hottest part of the day, as the leaves may scorch, especially the red orach.

Recommended

A. hortensis (orach) is a hardy annual that produces green, triangular leaves that resemble spades and tiny, insignificant greenish flowers. It can grow up to 5' tall and 12" wide. **'Rubra'** is slightly smaller in overall size, producing tiny reddish flowers and red triangular leaves.

A. patula (common orach, lamb's quarters) grows 36" tall and 12"

Use orach in salads and sandwiches.

wide, bearing spear-shaped, green leaves and insignificant flowers.

Harvesting and Processing

The leaves should be harvested throughout the growing season for fresh use. This herb does not dry or freeze well.

It's best to use the leaves as soon as possible, if not immediately, as they will only keep for one to two days, if kept sealed in plastic in the refrigerator.

Uses

The young leaves are delicious when used fresh in salads and sandwiches. The leaves are not aromatic, but they are tasty and reminiscent of spinach, only milder. The red-leaved cultivar also lends a pleasant color to dishes.

Medicinally, orach was said to treat sore throats and jaundice. It was also prescribed as a cure for menstrual problems.

Oregano · Marjoram
Origanum

Oregano and marjoram are two of the best known and most frequently used herbs. They are popular in stuffings, soups and stews, and no pizza is complete until it has been sprinkled with fresh or dried oregano leaves. If we had to point out a negative about *Origanum*, it would have to be that the selections with the best flavor have a low tolerance to cold winters, while the hardier ones are tougher and more vigorous but lack a lot of the flavor. What's the solution? Grow both, in fact grow all of them, because there are many to choose from, in different colors, strengths and forms.

Features
Other names: wild majoram, wild oregano
Parts used: leaves, flowers
Hardiness: zones 5–9

In Greek oros *means 'mountain' and* ganos *means 'joy and beauty,' so oregano translates as 'joy or beauty of the mountain.'*

Use these herbs to flavor oils; they can also be dried for later use.

Growing

Oregano and marjoram grow best in **full sun**. The soil should be of **poor to average fertility, neutral to alkaline** and **well drained**. The flowers attract pollinators to the garden. It's easiest to begin with starter plants, but you can also propagate with cuttings in late spring or grow them from seed. Starting seed indoors is best; plant the seedlings out when they reach at least 3" in height and the risk of frost has passed.

Marjoram is said to be a warming and relaxing herb, with antiseptic properties, useful when treating anxiety, insomnia or tension headaches.

Tips

These bushy perennials make a lovely addition to any border and can be trimmed to form low hedges. Oregano and majoram can also be grown in containers, making it easy to bring them in for the winter. They are a staple in herb gardens as well as vegetable gardens.

Recommended

O. majorana (marjoram, sweet marjoram) is upright and shrubby with light green, hairy leaves. It bears white or pink flowers in summer and can be grown as an annual where it is not hardy. It grows 24–36" tall and 12–18" wide (Zones 7–9).

O. vulgare (oregano) is a low, bushy plant that has hairy, grey-green leaves and bears white to pinkish flowers. Many other interesting cultivars of *O. vulgare* are available, including those with golden, variegated or curly leaves. Some of the most popular and interesting are: **'Aureum,'** which bears golden foliage with a mild flavor; **'Aureum**

Oregano in a mixed herb planter

O. vulgare 'Aureum' trimmed into a hedge

O. vulgare 'Aureum' with marigold and parsley

Crispum,' which produces rounded, crinkled leaves and **'Compactum,'** which has a mild flavor with a compact, dense growing habit. *O. v.* **subsp.** *hirtum* (Greek oregano) is the most flavorful of all the oreganos. It has a compact habit, hairy leaves and tiny white flowers. **'Variegata'** produces white and yellow variegated leaves. **'Zorba Red'** produces dark green, fragrant leaves and reddish purple sprays of flowers with hints of white (Zones 5–9).

Harvesting and Processing

All oregano and marjoram selections are best when used fresh. They dry well and retain much of their flavor, but fresh is far superior. The plants should be harvested just before they are in full flower. Hang bunches of stems in a cool and airy place to dry or chop the leaves finely, added to a little water and freeze into ice cube trays for later use. Strip the dry leaves from their stems into airtight containers for storing. The leaves can

Flowering oregano in a perennial bed (above); flowers close up (below)

also be chopped finely and added to softened butter. Once set up in the refrigerator, cut into pats or squares and store in airtight containers in the refrigerator. They will last for weeks.

Uses

Oregano's pungent flavor and aroma are suitable for pasta and rice dishes, dips and just about any dish with a tomato base. It can be used in meat dishes, sauces and dressings, vegetable dishes and herbal vinegars. It's a great addition to egg dishes, salsa, chili and cheese spreads.

Marjoram has a more delicate flavor, suitable for pasta sauces, vegetable dishes, pizza toppings and tomato sauces where a milder flavor is desired. It's commonly used in Italian, Mediterranean and Greek cuisine and is the perfect in breads and herbal oils and vinegars. The leaves and flowers can also be added to spice up potpourri.

O. vulgare 'Polyphant'

Parsley

Petroselinum

Though usually used as a garnish, parsley is rich in vitamins and minerals and is said to freshen the breath after garlic or onion-rich foods are eaten. Parsley is one of the main components of a traditional *bouquet garni* (French for garnished bouquet), along with rosemary, thyme, bay leaves and peppercorns. This herb is easy to grow, harvest and use in everyday meals. Parsley is also a helpful companion to other plants in the garden, including roses and tomatoes, not to mention pollinating insects and bees when in flower.

Fresh parsley is an indispensable, if ubiquitous, herb in cooking.

Features

Parts used: leaves, (roots but only for
P. crispum tuberosum)
Hardiness: zones 5–8

Growing

Parsley grows well in **full sun** or
partial shade. The soil should be
of **average to rich fertility, humus-
rich, moist** and **well drained**. Direct
sow seeds because the plants resent
transplanting. If you start seeds
early, use peat pots so the seedlings
can be potted or planted out without disruption.

*Parsley leaves make a tasty and
nutritious addition to salads. Tear
freshly picked leaves and sprinkle
them in your mixed greens.*

Tips

Parsley should be started where you
mean to grow it. Containers of pars
ley can be kept close to the house for
easy picking. The bright green leaves
and compact growth habit make
parsley a good edging plant for beds
and borders.

Recommended

P. crispum (curly parsley) forms a
clump of bright green, divided leaves.
This plant is biennial, but is usually
grown as an annual. 'Afro' produces
tightly curled, dark green foliage.
'Champion Moss Curled' has finely
cut, curled leaves. 'Clivi' is a dwarf
cultivar and 'Crispum' is a strongly
flavored, crinkly leaved selection.
'Dark' has very dark green leaves.
'Paramount' bears tightly curled,
dark green leaves and **var. *tuberosum***
(Hamburg parsley) produces
enlarged, edible roots. *P. crispum*
subsp. *neapolitanum* (Italian parsley, French parsley) produces flat
leaves with a stronger flavor.

Parsley fits right into a colorful contaner of annuals.

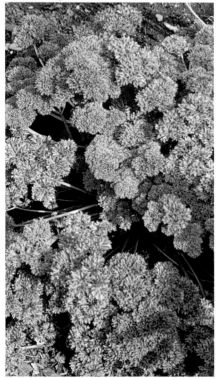

P. crispum

Harvesting and Processing

Parsley can be cut and used fresh throughout the growing season. It is most flavorful when used fresh. It can also be dried. It maintains its green color even after drying and will keep for months. For freezing, chop fresh leaves finely, mix with a little water and fill ice cube trays with the mix for later use. This can all be done throughout the season or just before hard frost in the fall, depending on how much parsley you require.

Parsley leaves can be fried and sprinkled over fish dishes for a little extra flavor and crunch.

Uses

Parsley has spent far too much time on the edge of a plate. It's earthy, fresh and crisp flavor is the perfect complement to so many dishes. Its mild flavor is also a great accompaniment to other herb mixtures. It works well with chervil, chives and tarragon, just to name a few. Fresh or dried, parsley was made for egg dishes including omelettes, sauces, mashed potatoes, salads, soups, pasta and vegetable dishes, especially those with poultry and fish. A tea can be made from steeping the leaves in boiling water. Parsley pesto, made with olive oil and pine nuts is a delightful addition to pastas, soups and breads.

Italian parsley is frequently used in Mediterranean and Middle Eastern cuisine because of its stronger flavor. Parsley is the main ingredient in a healthy and nutritious salad called tabbouleh, which also includes fresh mint. Parsley is also paired with coriander.

All parts of the plant are useful and beneficial for culinary and medicinal purposes. The roots can be boiled and eaten as a vegetable, particularly Hamburg parsley. The stems of Italian parsley can be finely chopped and used just as the leaves are used. The foliage from all parsley is rich in vitamin A, B and C.

Parsley has even been included in lotions for the scalp and hair before applying shampoo, which makes the hair very shiny and manageable. It is also used in herbal lotions to close large pores and as a freshener to reduce the puffiness around the eyes.

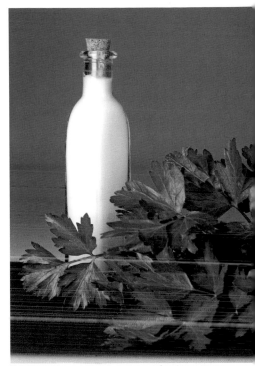

Parsley can be used in lotions to treat the skin and hair.

P. crispum neapolitanum

Perilla

Perilla

Perilla has been used for centuries as a medicinal plant in Chinese medicine and as an Asian culinary herb. With Asian cuisine as trendy as it is, not surprisingly so due to its simplicity, flavor and health benefits, you'll find yourself seeing perilla in the herb section of your local market and as part of a wonderful creation on the menu at your favorite restaurant. It's also experienced a resurgence as an ornamental. Breeders have introduced more decorative selections into the market, making perilla a highly sought after annual for gardeners. Whether you plant perilla for its ornamental value in the garden or for its use in the kitchen, this useful herb will become a regular addition to your garden landscape.

Perilla in a salad

Features

Other names: shiso, shisho, green shiso, red shiso, Japanese basil, aoshiso
Parts used: leaves, flowers, seeds
Hardiness: annual

Growing

Perilla prefers **full sun** or **partial shade**. The soil should be **fertile, moist** but **well drained**. Amending the soil with well-aged compost or manure is of added benefit. Perilla is a drought and shade tolerant plant. The plants should be pinched back regularly to maintain a bushy and dense habit. Perilla will self-sow in the right conditions.

Tips

Perilla is the perfect alternative to coleus and is an ideal complement to both brightly colored annuals and perennials in decorative containers and mixed beds. Perilla is also said to be a good companion plant to tomatoes, repelling "bad" insects. Planting this annual near or beside your vegetable garden or tomato plants is not only practical but also beautifies the immediate area.

Recommended

P. frutescens (perilla, shiso) is a vigorous annual with deeply toothed, mid-green leaves with flecks of purple. The leaves have a cinnamon-lemon flavor. Tiny white flowers are borne on spikes in summer, but this annual is grown more for its ornate, tasty and colorful foliage. **'Atropurpurea'** (beefsteak plant) produces deeply cut, crinkled leaves, burgundy red with pink flowers. **Var. crispa** (green shiso) has curly-edged leaves and **var. crispa rubra** (purple shiso) is very similar, but the foliage is burgundy red and the flowers are pink.

Perilla is well known for its tolerance to the summer heat and will easily compete with some of the most aggressive summer annuals available.

P. frutescens 'Magilla' (above); *P. frutescens* (below)

Most perilla selections will reach 36" in height and 24" in spread.

Harvesting and Processing

Perilla can be harvested and eaten at all stages of growth. If grown strictly for sprouting purposes, then the sprouts should be harvested at the juvenile stage and used fresh. If grown for the leaves, they should be picked during the growing season, because they are most flavorful when used fresh. They are usually gathered in bunches for cooking as greens or for used as nori or seaweed in Japanese cooking. The plant can be cut back by half mid-season, not only to encourage new, dense growth to be used later on, but also to harvest the finest leaves when they're most tender. The leaves can also be dried, just as most other herbs are dried. One method is to cut the leafy stems and tie them into bunches. Hang the bunches in a warm location with adequate air circulation. Once dry store the leaves in an airtight container. The leafy stems can also be dried on drying racks or in the microwave oven. Once ripe, the seeds can be shaken loose from the seedheads late in summer or early fall for planting the following year. Shake them into a paper bag and allow to dry. Once dry, store the seed in airtight containers in a cool location.

P. frutescens *'Magilla' is grown as an ornamental plant only, and should not be eaten. It can be grown in beds and containers, however, and looks stunning planted en masse.*

Uses

Having perilla leaves at your finger-tips is such a blessing since they're not always easy to find at the market, even with their burgeoning popularity. The sweet, light and spicy leaves can be used whole or chopped for garnishing, or battered and prepared as tempura. They can also be used in sushi. The seedpod stems are commonly used as a garnish when in flower. The leaves can also be pickled as they are in Japan, and served with rice. The small flower spikes are quite tasty and can be eaten fresh as an accompaniment to salads and soups. Sweet and sour dishes are the perfect platform for the seeds, as they are used for flavoring pickled plums and other sweet and sour treats.

Perilla seeds; *P. frutescens* 'Magilla' (below)

Perilla seed oil was recently found to contain omega–3, similar to flax seed oil — perfect for lowering bad cholesterol levels.

Rose

Rosa

Roses have an incredibly rich history in the culinary arts, crafting, medicine, the perfume industry and in folklore. Roses even have religious significance, because the petals are traditionally used to make rosary beads. In this book, we'll focus on the use of roses in the craft studio and the kitchen. Rose petals and hips are both edible. The petals can be highly fragrant, and that well-known scent is also very pleasurable to the palate. The hips are not only filled with flavor but are also bursting with vitamins, particularly vitamin C. In fact *Rosa rugosa* contains the highest amount of vitamin C of any plant in the world, containing up to 0.3 ounces of vitamin C per 3 ounces of rose hips. In all the ways they can be used, roses offer beauty and practicality.

Features

Parts used: flowers and hips
Hardiness: zones 3–9

Growing

Roses require **full sun to partial shade** in order to thrive. **Well drained, moist soil of average fertility** is best. The three species of roses listed here should be pruned in the summer after flowering.

Tips

Hardy roses are ideal for hiding unsightly embankments or slopes. Lower growing selections are great for groundcover and erosion control, and even low hedging or border plants. Roses work beautifully in mixed borders and small groupings for impact. Larger selections make beautiful specimens, particularly when in bloom.

Dried rose petals in potpourri

Rose water has cosmetic uses as well as culinary uses, particularly in Indian cuisine. It is also very tasty when added to vanilla ice cream.

Recommended

R. eglanteria (sweet briar rose, eglantine rose) is a species with a dense growth habit. It has arching to upright branches covered in hooked thorns. Its divided, apple-scented leaves have sticky, rust-colored hairs on the undersides and coarsely textured surfaces. Fragrant, single, pink flowers are produced in summer, surrounding bright yellow stamens, followed by scarlet-colored, oval hips. This species grows up to 8' tall and wide, and is hardy to zone 4.

R. gallica var. *officinalis* (apothecary's rose, crimson damask rose, Provins Rose, red rose of Lancaster) has a neat and rounded growth habit with dark green foliage and cupped to flat, semi-double, white-and-pink-striped flowers surrounding bright yellow stamens. The fragrant flowers are borne in spring or early summer,

R. gallica officinalis

followed by spherical, orange-red hips. It grows 3–4' tall and wide and is hardy to zone 3. **'Versicolor'** (Rosa Mundi) is a compact selection with pale pink flowers striped with deep reddish-pink.

R. rugosa (Rugosa rose, hedgehog rose, Japanese rose) is a vigorous species with coarsely textured, medium green leaves. It bears cupped, single, fragrant flowers in a medium shade of pink surrounding yellow stamens. Rounded, bright red hips are produced after the flowers. This species grows 3–8' tall and wide and is hardy to zone 2. **Var.** *alba* has white flowers, **var.** *rosea* has pink flowers and **var.** *rubra* has purple-red flowers.

Harvesting and Processing

Pick the petals throughout the blooming cycles and use fresh. Each species, variety, hybrid, cultivar and so on has a different flavor, so pick more than a few, combine and experiment for yourself. The darkest petals are said to be the most flavorful, but only you can be the judge of that. It is best to pick the flowers and petals mid-morning after any dew has evaporated but before the day becomes too hot. Select the flowers just as they fully open but before they begin to look spent and faded. The flowers can be cut at the stem, 4–5" from the flower base. Once the stem is cut, strip away any of the leaves, greenery and the stem.

The petals are best used when fresh. Ensure that they have been rinsed and are free of any insects or dirt. Remove the base or heel, which is often white or green, from each petal.

Pick the hips when they're in full color, ripe and plump but not soft and overripe. Only take the hip and not any part of the stem. Use the hips fresh or dried, and prepare them quickly after picking by slicing and removing the blossom end. They should then be cut in half, and the seed and fiber removed with a spoon.

To dry the hip halves, spread them out onto a screen in a cool, well-ventilated room. Store in airtight containers once dry.

Uses

Rose petals can be sprinkled onto salads for a fresh, flavor-packed addition. They can also be preserved in butter, syrup or vinegar, and they can be crystallized in sugar just as you would do with violets and borage flowers. Dried rose petals can be sprinkled into herbal teas for a slightly different flavor. Dried petals and whole flowers can also be used in a variety of crafts, including potpourri, herbal bath products, sachets and floral arrangements. An essential oil can also be extracted from this plant, but it is best purchased since it is a complicated process to produce the oil at home. The oil can be sprinkled into any craft you want to scent more strongly, or when something rose-scented needs refreshing.

Eat the hips fresh as a treat or add them to desserts and delicacies, whether dried or fresh.

The petals from any rose can be eaten, but the selections listed here are hardy, and disease- and pest-resistant. Not only do they not require spraying, but they should not be sprayed, with any type of fungicide or pesticide because their foliage is apt to burn.

R. gallica 'Versicolor' (Rosa Mundi) (above & below)

Rosemary

Rosmarinus

Even if you've only cooked once or twice in your life, or gardened once on a whim, chances are still pretty good that you've heard of rosemary. Native to the Mediterranean, rosemary has been used in cooking and medicine for thousands of years. One legend claims that rosemary won't grow taller than the height of Christ, or 5–6'. It is one of the few herbs that is bound to be in just about everyone's pantry and for good reason. Rosemary is a versatile and tasty herb, and it deserves a place in your kitchen and beauty regime.

Features

Parts used: leaves
Hardiness: zones 7–9, 6 with winter protection

Rosemary-scented soap

Growing

Rosemary prefers **full sun**, but tolerates partial shade. The soil should be of **poor to average fertility** and **well drained**. Do not let the soil surrounding rosemary dry out completely. In zones bordering on risky, mulch heavily around the plant with dead leaves for winter protection, and water in thoroughly. Rosemary can be grown from seed in early spring but it's much quicker and easier to begin with a starter plant, depending on the zone or length of season. Cuttings can also be taken in spring to start new plants.

Tips

Rosemary is best grown in a container as a specimen or within a mixed border or bed. Low-growing, spreading plants can be included in a rock garden or can be grown in hanging baskets. Upright forms can be trained as topiary specimens. The benefit to growing rosemary in a container is controlling its environment, because it can be a little finicky. It can be brought into the house before fall frost for winter harvest. For those lucky enough to live where rosemary is completely hardy, it can be implemented into the herb or vegetable garden as a companion to sage. Rosemary is an influential plant. It will draw in honey bees for pollination, repel carrot fly outdoors and moths indoors.

Recommended

R. officinalis is a dense, bushy evergreen shrub with narrow, dark green leaves. The habit varies somewhat between cultivars from strongly upright to prostrate and spreading. Flowers are usually in shades of blue, but pink-flowered cultivars are available (Zone 8). **'Arp'** is reliable to Zone 7 and even 6 with adequate winter protection. It bears grey-green foliage with good flavor and aroma. **'Blue Boy'** is a compact selection with a free flowering habit, great for growing indoors in a container. **'Blue Rain'** is a trailing selection suitable for hanging baskets and containers of all kinds. It can reach 18–24" in width due to its trailing stems, loaded with

A procumbent variety of *R. officinalis* (above); *R. officinalis* 'Prostratus' (below)

light blue flowers. **'Huntington Carpet'** is a low-growing, spreading cultivar, with dense foliage and heaps of flowers. **'Madeline Hill'** ('Hill Hardy') is a very winter hardy selection, named for noted Texas herbalist Madeline Hill. It bears pale bluish white flowers and broader leaves than 'Arp.' **'Majorca'** produces showy dark blue flowers with an upright to a trailing habit. **'Rexford'** ('Rex') is a stately selection with dark green leaves, a vigorous growth habit and deep blue flowers. This one is a favorite in the kitchen. **'Santa Barbara'** is a vigorous plant with a spreading habit and flowers earlier than most. **'Tuscan Blue'** is an upright, columnar selection with thick stems, succulent leaves and blue flowers. Its flavor and aroma are milder compared to other cultivars, but its ornamental value makes up for the difference. Cultivars are available that can survive in zone 6 in a sheltered location with winter protection. Plants rarely reach their mature size when grown in containers.

Harvesting and Processing
Harvest the leaves and flowers from this woody plant throughout the growing season or year-round when possible. Strip the fresh leaves from the trimmed stem tips and use as is or dry in paper bags and stored in airtight containers. Preserve the fresh

leaves by chopping them and freezing them in an ice cube tray with water, or by storing sprigs in foil in the freezer. The flavor and aroma of the foliage is best before the plant flowers. Individual stems or sprigs can be cut during the summer; harvest all of the stems before hard frost, dry or freeze for year round use. Collect and store the flowers just as you would the leaves. If growing rosemary indoors over the winter, use it sparingly because it is receiving less light and producing fewer leaves.

Uses

The needle-like leaves of rosemary are used to flavor chicken, pork, lamb, rice, tomato and egg dishes. The leaves can be chopped and sprinkled over salads, and fresh leafy stems can be laid on cuts of roasting meat. Add fresh leaves to herb butters, sugars and oils, cool summer drinks, marinades for fish and poultry and sauces for vegetables. The newest growth should be used for cooking while the older growth is ideal for potpourri, sachets and crafts.

Rosemary can also be used in handmade soaps, lotions, hair conditioners and shampoos and skin cleansers.

Medicinally, rosemary is said to have antiseptic and antibacterial properties. It is thought to treat colds, flu, fatigue and headaches. It has been used in tinctures to treat depression and anxiety. Infused into a massage oil, it is beneficial for rheumatic and muscular pain and is great in a bath to alleviate aching joints and exhaustion.

Try adding rosemary to a martini for a flavor twist.

After a few years, rosemary will become thin and lanky. Plan on propagating or starting over about every three years or so.

Rosemary pruned into a standard form

Safflower

Carthamus

Safflower is a herb many may have heard of, but they often don't know where it comes from or what benefits it has to offer. Safflower is an odd-looking plant, there is no doubt, it's not one that people immediately think of when you say stunning ornamental. It is, however, a useful and tough little plant that possesses attributes useful to the crafter and artist. It's other properties are all just gravy.

Features
Other names: American saffron, false saffron
Parts used: flowers, seeds, oil
Hardiness: annual

Growing

Safflower prefers a location in **full sun**. The soil should be **light** and **well drained**. It is very tolerant of dry conditions. Seed is the best form of propagation.

Tips

Safflower is most effective when planted in large groups. Everlasting gardens are a common place to find safflower because of its use as a dried flower for crafts and arrangements. It can be planted in mixed beds and borders with other annuals or perennials. Because of its sparse growth habit, it doesn't work well in containers.

Recommended

C. tinctorius is an erect annual that produces simple, gray-green foliage sparsely along tall stems. Atop those stems emerge thistle-like flowerheads composed of large green bracts that resemble a tightly closed flower, topped with a puff of bright yellow petals poking out of the tip. It grows 12–24" tall and 12" wide. **'Lasting White,'** bears creamy white blossoms, **'Orange Ball'** has orange flowers and **'Summer Sun'** has bright yellow flowers.

Harvesting and Processing

Cut the flowers soon after they've opened. Hang stems to dry, either in bunches or on a drying rack. Once dry, gently strip the petals from the bulby bracts and store in airtight containers.

Uses

Crafters, but more specifically textile artists and weavers, love safflower for its use as a dye. Simply steeping the

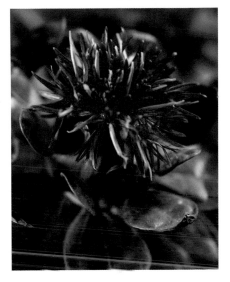

petals in boiling water transfers the warm tones into the water which can be used for dying fabrics, yarn, thread and floss. Safflower has even been used as a food colorant. Add the petals to potpourri for color.

Cosmetically, the dye is used for herbal make-up and hair color.

Medicinally, safflower is very versatile. A tea produced from steeping the petals in boiling water is said to reduce fevers. It can also act as a mild laxative. Applied externally, lotions with safflower are useful to treat bruises, skin irritations and inflammation.

In the kitchen, safflower petals can be used to replace saffron, and to add color to rice and egg dishes.

Safflower oil is produced from the seeds. Used for cooking, the oil is an important part of a low cholesterol diet.

Saffron

Crocus

Saffron has been an important herb for thousands of years. It is highly valued among cooks and chefs; it also offers the artist or crafter a useful, natural dye. Saffron was first brought to Europe by the Crusaders in the Middle Ages. It has been highly valued for the delicate flavor that the rusty-yellow stigmas impart into a variety of dishes. The flowers themselves are beautiful in late fall. It only takes a pinch of the stigmas to delicately flavor a dish such as risotto, so thankfully a little saffron goes a long way.

Growing

Saffron prefers to grow in locations with **full sun to partial shade**. The soil should be **rich, very well drained and dry**. Plant corms 4–6" deep in spring for the best results. Saffron blooms well the first year but sparsely thereafter. It is important to divide

Features

Other names: saffron crocus
Parts used: flower stigmas
Hardiness: zones 6–8

the offsets from the older corms for transplanting to renew your crop every 1 to 2 years. In zones colder than 6, dig up the corms and store indoors for winter before the ground freezes. Store the corms in dry peat moss or sand in a cool and dry place (e.g. basement). Water the newly replanted corms only in spring after all risk of frost has passed, and again once the new foliage emerges in fall.

Tips
Plant saffron en masse, in drifts or mixed borders for late season color and interest. Raised beds and rock gardens are ideal locations, as are naturalized, grassy areas or meadows.

Recommended
C. sativus produces 1–5 wide fragrant, purple flowers with dark purple veins, dull green, grass-like leaves, central purple filaments and yellow anthers. Its long, three-branched, deep rusty red stigmas or styles are the saffron threads used in cooking and dying. This species will only grow up to 3" tall and wide.

Harvesting and Processing
Pick the stigmas carefully from the center of each flower, and store them for 2 to 3 years. Harvest mid-morning, on a sunny day, when the flowers are fully open and the stigmas are still fresh. Dry them in a warm location and store dried stigmas in an airtight container.

Uses
Two dozen corms will generate enough saffron to use at home. With each consecutive year, the corms will increase in number, the size of the planting will grow larger with more spicy stigmas. Every 4 to 6 years,

Saffron threads visible at the center of each flower

divide and replant the corms once the foliage has faded to prevent overcrowding, which can lead to a decrease in flowering

Steep saffron threads in hot water, broth or milk for about 20 minutes, depending on your recipe. Add the threads and liquid early in the cooking or baking process for maximum flavor and color.

The flavor of saffron transforms many dishes, including potatoes, mussels, white fish, paella, baked goods and even ice cream. It complements asparagus, chicken, eggs, mushrooms and spinach especially well.

To use saffron as a dye, use a mordant such as alum to "fix" the color because saffron is water-soluble. Buddhist monks have dyed their robes with saffron for thousands of years. You can dye almost any natural fiber with saffron, even wood.

Don't confuse *Crocus sativus* with *Colchicum*, a highly poisonous fall-blooming crocus. *Colchicum*, sometimes referred to as autumn crocus or meadow saffron, is beautiful but must not be eaten.

Sage
Salvia

Rosemary, sage and thyme make an everlasting trio of herbs. They work incredibly well together but are equally as tasty individually. Sage certainly isn't lacking in the looks department. Each species, hybrid and cultivar is unique and attractive and beautiful enough to plant strictly for its ornamental value. I usually add common sage or tricolor to my silver- and grey-themed pots, for their dense growth habit, fresh and spicy aroma and unique appeal. They're also tough as nails, and I can eat them! Talk about the perfect equation; pretty plus practical plus tasty equals a great herb.

Features

Parts used: leaves
Hardiness: zones 4–9

Growing

Sage prefers **full sun** but tolerates
light shade. The soil should be of
average fertility and **well drained**.
These plants benefit from a light
mulch of compost each year. They
are drought tolerant once established. Sage can be started from seed
in spring but it's much quicker and
easier to start with new plants.

Tips

Sage is an attractive plant for the
border, adding volume to the middle
of the border or as an attractive edging or feature plant near the front.
Sage can also be grown in mixed
planters or as a specimen so it can
be brought indoors in the winter
months for year round use.

Sage butter with dried and fresh sage

Salvia comes from the Latin
salvere, "to save or to heal,"
hence this herb's connection to
good health and long life.

Recommended

S. elegans is a soft-stemmed plant with
a branching form. It bears mid-green,
mildly pineapple-scented leaves and
bright scarlet flower spikes. It can grow
up to 6' tall but does so rarely. '**Golden
Delicious**' has soft gold foliage that
provides an interesting color contrast
to its vibrant red flowers. '**Scarlet Pineapple**' (pineapple sage) produces leaves
strongly scented of pineapple when
crushed and larger flowers than the
species (Zones 8–10).

S. fruticosa (Greek sage) is a bushy,
evergreen shrub with branched stems,
mid-green foliage and purple, pink
or white flowers. It grows up to 4' tall
and 36" wide (Zones 8–10).

S. lavandulifolia (narrow-leaved
sage, Spanish sage) is a woody based
perennial with long stems clothed in
woolly leaves and blue to violet flowers. It grows up to 24" tall and wide
(Zones 5–9).

S. officinalis 'Tricolor' planted with cilantro, basil and chives

Sage has been used since ancient Greek times, and perhaps even earlier, as a medicinal and culinary herb and continues to be widely used for both those purposes today.

Purple sage mixed with ornamental sorrel and pepper

S. officinalis (common sage) is a woody, mounding plant with soft, grey-green leaves. Spikes of light purple flowers appear in early and mid-summer. It grows 24–36" tall and wide. Many cultivars with attractive foliage are available, including the compact, golden-leaved '**Aurea**', the silver-leaved '**Berggarten,**' the yellow-margined '**Icterina,**' the purple-leaved '**Purpurea**' and the purple-green and cream variegated '**Tricolor,**' whose new growth has a pink flush (Zones 5–8).

S. sclarea (clary sage) is an erect, branchy perennial or biennial with toothed or notched leaves. From spring to summer it bears purple, pink or violet flowers with prominent lilac bracts. It grows 36" tall and 12" wide (Zones 5–9).

Harvesting and Processing

Fresh leaves are always best and should be harvested before the plant flowers, unless the flowers are being pinched off throughout the growing season. The leaves can be chopped finely, mixed with a little water and frozen into ice cube trays for year-round use. They can also be dried by hanging bunches loosely on drying racks, but never in direct sunlight. Once the leaves are dry, strip them from the stems and store in airtight containers.

S. elegans

Uses

Sage is perhaps best known as a flavoring for stuffing, but it has a great range of uses, including in soups, stews, sausages and dumplings. Sage will counteract the richness of certain foods and aids in digestion. Sage can be combined with other herbs, especially tarragon and marjoram, or used on its own when cooking almost any type of meat dish.

When used for medicinal purposes, sage is used to restore energy. It's even said to improve a bad memory. It is commonly recommended that students drink sage tea while studying to help in fact-retention. It's an important ingredient in naturally based mouthwashes and gargles. Cosmetically it is used in hair tonics to prevent the hair follicles from losing their pigment and going grey. Sage has even been used to whiten teeth by rubbing a fresh leaf over them every day. It's used in cleansing lotions, hair rinses and deodorants.

S. officinalis

S. officinalis 'Icterina' mixed with Italian parsley, thyme and tarragon

Salad Burnet

Sanguisorba

This hardy self seeder adds a cucumber flavor to your favorite fresh salads. The scalloped leaves often prompt a "what is this?" response. Try adding the young leaves to tabouli and tzatziki, a Mediterranean yogurt cucumber dip, and use it to garnish food that needs a hint of summer flavor. It also has the ability to freshen your breath after you have eaten your favorite garlic-rich foods.

Features
Other names: garden burnet, Italian burnet, Italian pimpernel, official burnet
Parts used: leaves
Hardiness: zones 3–8

Growing
Salad burnet is best grown in a location with **full sun** or **partial shade**. It requires reasonably **rich, well drained soil** that is **moist** and **amended with organic matter**. It can be started from seed in spring. It should be cut back as soon as the flowers begin to emerge to ensure a dense crop of foliage.

Tips
This pretty ornamental is well suited to a mixed border, herb garden, raised bed or vegetable garden. It also works well as a border plant in formal and informal settings.

Recommended
S. minor (*Poterium sanguisorba*) is a clump-forming perennial that grows 8–18" tall. It bears deeply toothed leaflets and long stems topped with clusters of rounded, deep cerise and green flowerheads.

Harvesting and Processing
The leaves of this plant should be used fresh for culinary purposes because they do not dry well. The ice cube method is the best way to preserve the fresh flavor and texture of the leaves for year-round use. Drying is possible as a last resort and is only useful if the leaves will be cooked and not if they will be used to flavor drinks or fresh in salads and other cold foods. Store the dried leaves in airtight containers and discard the stems.

Salad burnet imparts a cucumber flavor to summer drinks.

Uses
The fresh leaves from this herb taste nutty and a little like cucumber, a flavor that works well in soups, casseroles, salads, herbal vinegars and cheese. The leaves are also very tasty in cabbage dishes such as coleslaw. Floating a few fresh leaves in cold, summer drinks and wine punches will add a pleasant cucumber flavor to the mix. The leaves can also be used as a garnish. They also make a great substitute for cress in sandwiches.

Medicinally, salad burnet is said to help cure rheumatism and promote perspiration when taken as a tea. An infusion of salad burnet, when cooled and applied to the face, will help to clear the skin. Muslin bags of salad burnet steeped in bath water will leave you refreshed and invigorated. Herbalists prescribe it to treat diarrhea and to reduce inflammation. The leaves can be applied to sores, cankers and burns as well.

Savory

Satureja

The savories are strong, peppery flavored
herbs. Well known for flavoring salami,
they are added to a wide variety of
vegetable and meat dishes. Summer
savory is considered to have the most
refined flavor of the two savories, but
winter savory is favored among gardeners
because it's a perennial herb. Winter savory is
known to have a strong flavor that is sometimes
difficult to blend into most cuisines. Summer
savory is quite the opposite. Experimenting
is always recommended with herbs, so try
them both.

Savory is ideal for flavoring sauces.

Features

Parts used: leaves
Hardiness: zones 5–9

Growing

Savories grow best in **full sun**. The soil should be of **poor to average fertility, neutral to alkaline** and **well drained**. The flowers attract bees, butterflies and other pollinators to the garden. Savory benefits from a prompt start from seed indoors approximately one month before last frost in the spring or with seedlings once the risk of frost has passed.

Summer savory leaves are reputed to relieve bee stings when rubbed on the sore spot.

Tips

These low-growing plants are attractive in the front of beds and borders. They don't like too much moisture in their soil, so they are better suited to the rock garden than the vegetable garden. When the soil's been prepared adequately, savory can also become an integral part of your herb garden. It will also thrive in a container, making it easy to take indoors for the winter.

Recommended

S. hortensis (summer savory) is a bushy, aromatic annual with narrow leaves. It bears white or pink flowers in summer. The species grows up to 12" tall and wide. **'Aromata'** is a compact form with a higher oil content in its leaves, resulting in more aromatic and flavorful leaves. **'Midget'** is a bushier and taller selection with a high essential oil content.

S. montana (winter savory) is a semi-evergreen subshrub that is treated like a perennial. It has narrow, dark green leaves that stay on the

The delicate blooms of *S. hortensis* (above); *S. montana* (below)

plant through early winter and are very strong and pungent. Pink or purple flowers are produced for most of summer. This species grows 16" tall and only 8–10" wide (Zones 5–9).

Harvesting and Processing

The leaves can be pinched from the stems throughout the growing season for use when fresh. They can also be dried successfully in a cool, airy place. The leafy stems should be harvested before they flower. Once dry, the leaves can be easily stripped from the stems and stored in airtight containers. The leaves can also be frozen for later use, either by the ice cube tray method or by wrapping leafy stems in foil. The fresh flavor is longer lasting when the leaves are frozen in cubes however. The foil method will only maintain the leaf flavor for a few weeks.

Young *S. hortensis* plants

Uses

Both types of savory can be used in the same way, just remember that a little goes a long way. Finely chopped leaves, whether fresh or dried, can be added to bean and legume dishes, fish and meat dishes and to cream or white sauces. It's an ideal herb for flavoring sauces and the perfect substitute for black pepper. Savory butter is very tasty and freezes well.

Medicinally, savory is said to benefit those with respiratory problems, flatulence and colic. Savory tea is useful when going through a cleanse because its known to purify the system. The addition of savory to food, especially legume dishes, will aid in digestion.

Cosmetically, savory has a tonic effect on the skin and can be steeped in a hot bath for this purpose. In an infusion, it can be used to freshen breath as well.

Planting savory seeds closely to plant seeds may inhibit the germination of those seeds.

Scented Geranium

Pelargonium

It's important not to confuse scented geraniums with the more traditional zonale or ivy leaved geranium, or with perennial geraniums. While they all emit a unique odor, some smell better than others. For our purposes, scented geraniums are most familiar to gardeners by the names mosquito plant or citronella plant, those being only two of the many, many selections on the market. Unfortunately there is no room to list all of the wonderful scented geraniums available, but we will list some of our personal favorites. Scented geraniums have much more to offer than just repelling mosquitoes anyway, and they're incredibly easy to grow.

Features

Other names: scented pelargonium
Parts used: leaves
Hardiness: tender perennial mostly
treated as an annual; zones 9–11

Growing

Geraniums prefer **full sun** but tolerate partial shade, although they may not bloom as profusely in shade. The soil should be **fertile** and **well drained**.

Geraniums are slow to grow from seed, but if you want to start your own from seed, start them indoors in early winter and cover them with clear plastic to maintain humidity until they germinate. Once the seedlings have three or four leaves, transplant them into individual 3–4" pots. Keep your transplants in bright locations because they need lots of light to maintain a compact shape.

Tips

Scented geraniums blend beautifully with other annuals and perennials, in mixed beds, containers and herb gardens, and are especially effective when planted in large groups for added impact.

Recommended

P. **species** and cultivars is a large group of geraniums that have coarsely textured, fuzzy, deeply lobed or serrated, ornate leaves that emit a scent when rubbed or bruised. The scents are grouped into the categories of rose, mint, citrus, fruit, spice and pungent. In the following list, a parent of each cultivar is indicated in parentheses. Some cultivars, such as **'Apple'** (*P. odoratissimum*), readily self-seed and stay true to form, but most must be propagated by cuttings

Scented geranium in potpourri

to retain their ornamental and fragrant qualities. Many cultivars have variegated leaves. Intensely scented cultivars include **'Chocolate-Mint'** and **'Fair Ellen'** (*P. quercifolium*), **'Lemon'** (*P. crispum*), **'Nutmeg'** and **'Variegated Nutmeg'** (*P.* x *fragrans*), **'Old-fashioned Rose'** (*P. graveolens*), **'Peppermint'** (*P. tomentosum*), **'Prince Rupert'** (*P. crispum*), **'Rober's Lemon Rose'** (*P. graveolens*) and **'Strawberry'** (*P.* x *scarboroviae*).
P. x *asperum* **'Lady Plymouth'** produces rose and eucalyptus-scented, variegated foliage and lavender pink flowers, while **'Citronella'** (*'Citrosum,'* mosquito plant) has lemon-scented, coarsely-textured foliage.

Unique cultivars are also available, with more subtle aromas, including

'**Pretty Polly**' or almond geranium, '*M. Ninon,*' or apricot geranium. *P.* x *capitatum* '**Attar of Roses**' emits a splendid aroma, reminiscent of roses. '**Clorinda**' has a pleasant scent with a hint of eucalyptus while the species *P. grossularioides* smells like coconut. '**Pungent Peppermint**' is a strongly aromatic plant with an upright, vigorous habit.

Harvesting and Processing

Fresh leaves can be picked throughout the growing season for multiple uses. In late summer or early fall, cut the plants back by half if they are being grown in containers so they can be brought indoors in winter. Bring the cropped plants inside before a hard frost. Gather cuttings either for propagation or for drying. Place the plants in a bright location indoors throughout the winter, and expect a little growth. Cut off any stretched, weak stems. Keep the plants more dry than wet, and increase your watering as spring approaches. Begin fertilizing in early spring, but wait until the last frost has passed before moving them outside. In milder zones, possibly zone 9, the containers can be left in a garage or shelter to overwinter as long as the temperature in the shelter won't go below 32/34° F. Don't let plants dry out completely, and check with your local garden center on the hardiness of your selections.

Dry the leaves by hanging them in bunches on drying racks or on screens. Once dry, strip the leaves from the stems and store in airtight containers. The leaves will also last for weeks frozen whole in a layer or two of foil.

Scented geraniums can have unconventional (above) or conventional uses (below).

Uses

The leaves are commonly used with other aromatics in potpourri, sachets and herbal bags for the bath and to scent toiletries, herb pillows and air fresheners. Leafy stems can be integrated in herbal wreaths and dried floral arrangements. Fresh, leafy stems and flowers can be added to fresh flower arrangements for its scent and texture.

Most scented geraniums add a unique flavor to drinks and desserts. Whole, fresh leaves can be dropped into drinks, including tea, for flavoring but are generally not eaten. The leaves can be used to flavor cake batters and puddings but should be removed before baking. They're also useful to flavor ice cream, sorbet, sauces, fruit punch, herbal vinegar and gelatins. The flowers are also edible.

Soapwort

Saponaria

Soapwort is a herb with history. For those who have wondered what some used for soap before there was soap, there was soapwort. The stems and root contain a high concentration of saponins, which, when extracted, work just as a commercial soap does. There are no current medicinal purposes for this plant and no culinary purposes to speak of, yet it's still a useful plant and as an added benefit, it's beautiful in the landscape. It can be grown and over-wintered in decorative containers and blends beautifully with bolder-leaved plants, including pulmonaria and hosta.

Features
Other names: Bouncing Bet
Parts used: leafy stems, rhizomes or roots
Hardiness: zones 2–8

S. officinalis 'Rosea Plena'

Growing

Soapwort prefers to grow in **full sun** or **partial shade**. **Neutral to alkaline soil** that is **well drained** and **moist** is best. Plant starter plants or sow seed in early spring once the risk of frost has passed and the soil has warmed. It can be propagated by softwood cuttings and division. It can become invasive. Do not plant soapwort close to ponds because of its potential to poison fish.

Tips

Soapwort is a worthy border perennial when mixed with other perennials and annuals, as well as ornamental shrubs. It can also be integrated nicely into the herb garden.

Recommended

S. officinalis is a rhizomatous perennial with narrow, oval leaves up to 4" long on tall stems. It bears pale pink flowers in clusters from mid-summer to fall. It grows 12–36" tall and 24" wide. **'Dazzler'** produces leaves splashed with creamy splotches. **'Rubra Plena'** has double, deep pink flowers.

Harvesting and Processing

The leafy stems should be harvested in the summer and throughout the growing season. The rhizomes or roots can be harvested in late fall. Both the leafy stems and roots can be dried for later use.

Uses

Soapwart was used prior to the production of soap in the 1800s, and is still used today in the Middle East and in museums for cleaning tapestries, wooden furniture and pictures of all kinds. Dried soapwort can be used for washing delicate items. It can be used as a shampoo, but be careful not to get it into your eyes. To make soapwort shampoo, combine ½ oz of crushed, dried soapwort root or two large handfuls of roughly chopped, fresh stems with 1½ pints of water. Soak dried stems overnight to make them easier to use. In an enamel pot, bring water and soapwort to a boil and simmer for 20 minutes. Allow to cool and strain. It will keep for up to a week when stored in an airtight container. This can also be used as a skin rinse to relieve itchiness.

Sorrel

Rumex

This may not be one of the most well-known herbs, but it deserves wider use. It's not only a lovely, dense plant, but its tangy, zesty leaves can be used in soups, salads and many other dishes. It also holds its place in history based not only on its culinary uses but also on its medicinal value. Written about since the 14th century, sorrel was one of the most popular herbs in France and Belgium, used chiefly as a cooking herb. Just as it is used today, sorrel is a great addition to simple dishes including omelets and other egg recipes, or served as a side dish, similar to cooked spinach. If you're fond of lemony flavored herbs, then sorrel may just be the next one to experiment with.

A facial bath made by steeping sorrel leaves in warm water

Features
Parts used: leaves
Hardiness: zones 4–8

Growing
Sorrel should be grown in **full sun**, but it tolerates partial shade. A **moist, rich, acidic soil** with great **drainage** is best. The seeds should be sown in late spring. Remove flowerheads as they appear, because the plants can go to seed quite rapidly.

Tips
Sorrel is the perfect addition to any herb or culinary garden for its multiple uses. Sorrel can also adorn ornamental beds when mixed with various perennials, annuals and shrubs.

French sorrel is a fine companion to oregano in the garden, keeping both plants healthier over time and free of pests.

Recommended
R. acetosa (common sorrel) is a hardy perennial that produces large, mid-green leaves with a mild flavor. Small flowers are produced but are considered to be inconspicuous. This species will grow 2–4' tall and 12–24" wide.

R. scutatus (French sorrel, buckler-leaf sorrel), the main ingredient in sorrel soup, has smaller leaves that are less bitter, with a hint of lemon. It produces shield-shaped, mid-green leaves and inconspicuous flowers. It will grow 6–18" tall and 24" wide. **'Silver Shield'** has silvery green leaves and only grows 6–18" tall but up to 4' wide, making for a good ground cover in the right zone.

Harvesting and Processing
Pick the fresh leaves throughout the growing season; they are most flavorful when fresh. Once the growing season is over, in colder zones, the leaves can be harvested and either frozen whole in foil or dried on wire racks in a cool, dark place with adequate air circulation. Once dry, store in airtight containers.

Sorrel can be grown in your vegetable garden (above); sorrel that has gone to seed (below)

Uses

Eat sorrel just as you would spinach. When used in egg dishes, the sharp flavor of the leaves is mellowed and balanced. French sorrel is still commonly used to make sorrel soup, a puree of the leaves. A sauce made from the leaves is a delicious accompaniment to poultry and fish dishes, boiled potatoes and lamb. Young leaves can be tossed into salads and tucked into sandwiches for a bit of bite.

Sorrel, like spinach, should not be cooked in aluminum cookware. Medicinally, sorrel is said to cool fevers and aid in digestion. Cosmetically, sorrel is listed as one of the

Do not consume sorrel in great quantity or too frequently, as large doses can be poisonous. People with kidney disease, rheumatism, gout or kidney stones should not take sorrel internally.

R. acetosa (above); R. acetosella or sheep sorrel (center); sorrel in a bed of mixed herbs (below)

herbs that retards the signs of aging because of its calcium content. It can be used in a facial steambath to help prevent the onset of wrinkles and to heal acne; it can also be blended into handmade facial lotions for dry and sensitive skin or for its astringent properties. If taken in tea form, it's said to help clear the skin.

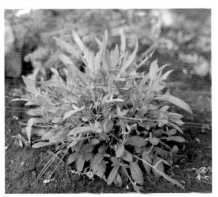

In locations with excessively warm summers, sorrel leaves can become bitter as the season progresses. Mulching around the base of the plants helps to keep the soil cooler and improves the flavor of the leaves.

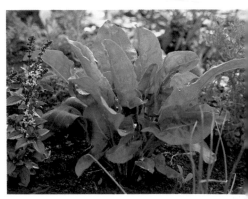

Sheep sorrel, *R. acetosella*, has ornamental value, but should not be consumed by humans.

Stevia

Stevia

Stevia is unique among other herbs. This plant isn't used to flavor food, to make crafts, to scent cosmetics and bath products or to fill sachets. It isn't used for anything but as a herbal sugar substitute, but this one-use plant is about to become revolutionary. This remarkable plant contains steviol glycosides, compounds that are up to 300 times sweeter than sugar but without the calories. Stevia powder can be bought at health food stores, but you can also grow your own at home for use as a sugar substitute. It's relatively easy to grow and will help you to reduce your processed sugar intake. How can that be bad?

Features
Other names: sweet honey leaf, sweetleaf, sugarleaf
Parts used: leaves
Hardiness: tender perennial that is mostly treated as an annual

Growing

Stevia prefers **full sun to partial shade**. Since glycoside synthesis is reduced at or just before flowering, delaying flowering allows more time for glycoside accumulation. Pinching out emerging flowers will alleviate this situation. The soil should be **well drained, moist** and **fertile**. Seeding stevia can be difficult because of poor germination rates. It is easier to start with a new plant, which will result in a quicker harvest.

Tips

Stevia integrates well into mixed beds and borders as edging, and has the most impact planted in groups. Growing stevia in containers is best for those who plan on bringing it indoors for the winter. One to three plants should supply the average person with enough leaves year-round to use as a refined sugar substitution.

Recommended

S. rebaudiana can grow 24–36" tall and 12–24" wide. It produces hairy stems covered in dark green, toothed leaves. White, tubular flowers are produced mid-summer. The leaves are not aromatic but are sweet to the taste. Dried leaves are even sweeter.

Harvesting and Processing

Harvest the leaves before flowering to ensure the highest concentration of glycosides. The fresh leaves can be cut and used immediately, but the sweetness increases exponentially when the leaves are dried. Spread leaves out on screens or racks until completely dry. Once dry, store them in airtight containers.

Powdered stevia leaves (above); stevia ready for harvest (below)

Uses

Powdered stevia leaves are primarily used as a sweetener in tea and coffee. Stevia does not break down when heated, so it can be used in cooking or baking without a problem. Stevia will not carmelize or crystallize; however, so some recipes may not work with stevia as a sweetener. The stems are also edible and sweet but not nearly as sweet as the leaves.

Sweet Cicely

Myrrhis

Sweet cicely has a surprising variety of culinary uses because all parts of the plant are edible. It is also a very pretty shade plant for the garden. Historically, sweet cicely was used for medicinal purposes but is now rarely used in this way. The boiled root was once said to be a tonic for the elderly and teenagers. As most things change over time, so did the uses for this herb. Somehow neglected over the generations, sweet cicely lost its place in the herb and vegetable garden, but is now making an appearance once again. Its versatility may just surprise you.

Features

Other names: garden myrrh
Parts used: leaves, flowers, seeds, roots
Hardiness: zones 3–8

Growing

Sweet cicely grows best in **partial or light shade**, but tolerates full sun in a sufficiently moist soil. The soil should be of **average fertility, damp** and **well drained**. Plants self-seed but not invasively.

Tips

This beautiful plant deserves to be included in shade gardens and borders as well herb gardens. Sweet cicely has a long taproot and does not grow well in a container unless the pot is deep enough for the root to grow. Placed in a partly to fully shaded location, it will grow but not as vigorously as it might in the ground.

Recommended

M. odorata forms a clump of soft, fragrant, fern-like leaves. It bears airy clusters of tiny, white flowers in spring. The flowers are followed by shiny, brown seeds. It grows 1–4' tall and 2–4' wide.

Harvesting and Processing

Pick young leaves throughout the growing season for fresh use. Harvest the seeds when unripe (green) or once ripe (dark brown). The leaves and seeds do not freeze or dry well at all so they should both be used fresh. The seeds will last for a short time if stored in airtight containers. Dig up the roots for drying in the fall, but only after the top of the plant has died back.

M. odorata in full bloom

Uses

Sweet cicely leaves are an excellent sugar replacement. They can be chopped and added to salads, soups, stews or mixed into yogurt. A handful of leaves added to stewed rhubarb will reduce the need for sugar by half.

The roots can be eaten raw, chopped up and mixed with salad greens or cooked or roasted like parsnips.

The slightly oily seeds are delicately spicy, reminiscent of licorice or anise, and are tasty when sprinkled into salads. The seeds can also be crushed and added to ice cream, pies and other fruity dishes.

Sweet cicely has also been used for medicinal purposes over the years. It was said to treat rheumatic complaints, stomach complaints and improve digestion.

Sweet Woodruff

Galium

Sweet woodruff is a vigorous groundcover for partially shaded, moist gardens. Charming, sweetly scented, star-shaped blossoms begin to emerge in early spring above a mat of low-growing, deep green foliage pretty enough to stand on its own. This groundcover is stunning when grown around broad-leaved, foliage perennials. The decorative foliage is not only beautiful to look at, but is also a treat for the senses.

Features

Parts used: flowers and leaves
Hardiness: zones 3–8

The wiry, creeping habit of sweet woodruff makes it an excellent groundcover; it is particularly effective under trees. The white flowers seem to glow at dusk in late spring.

Growing
This plant prefers **partial shade**.
Sweet woodruff will grow well in
full shade but with greatly dimin-
ished flowering. The leaves are prone
to sun scorch in strong, full sun. **Soil**
should be **humus rich** and **evenly
moist**. Divide plants in spring or fall.

Tips
Sweet woodruff is a perfect woodland groundcover. It forms a beautiful green carpet and loves the same
conditions in which azaleas and rho-
dodendrons thrive. Shear back after
blooming to encourage plants to fill
in with foliage and crowd out weeds.

Recommended
G. odoratum is a low, spreading
groundcover. Clusters of star-shaped,
white flowers are borne in late spring.
Emerald green, lance-shaped leaves
are borne with tiny, marginal prick-
les. The tiny, white flowers contrast
beautifully with the perky, dense foliage, creating a bright carpet suitable
for any shady border.

Harvesting and Processing
Pick the flowers and leaves throughout the summer and dry for later

Sweet woodruff sachet (above); *G. odoratum* (below)

use; the scent intensifies once dry.
Dry the leaves and flowers on screens,
in paper bags or on drying racks.
Once dry, store in airtight containers.

Uses
In parts of Europe, the fragrant foliage was once added to white wine
in May, creating what was called
May wine. Still produced today, May
wine is made of Moselle, sugar and
sparkling water or champagne, and
flavored with sweet woodruff. The
flowers also make a tasty addition to
salads, but only in very small quantities; large amounts may cause stomach upset. This herb is still used
medicinally today to relieve stomach
ailments when ingested in a tea form.

Tansy

Tanacetum

Tansies are very dependable members of the daisy family. These hard-working flowers will bloom over a long period and will stay orderly after being pinched back in May or June. Included in this flower group are feverfew, useful to many migraine sufferers, and *Pyrethrum*, which has insecticidal attributes. Aside from their dependability, versatility and usefulness, tansies are just beautiful plants. Some gardeners aren't very keen on their aroma, but we find it irresistible.

Tansy flowers and leaves can be steeped to make a dye.

Features

Parts used: leaves, flowers
Hardiness: zones 3–9

Growing

Tansies grow best in **full sun**. Any **well drained soil** is suitable, but very fertile soil may encourage invasive growth. Deadheading prolongs the blooming period. Divide in spring as needed to control spread and maintain plant vigour.

Tips

Use tansies in borders, rock gardens, wildflower gardens, cottage gardens and meadow gardens. Most species are quite civilized, but *T. vulgare* can become quite invasive. Grow the less invasive cultivar, or grow the species in planters and remove the flowers before the seeds ripen. A few of the species grow very tall and become a little lanky. Supporting the stems with a wire grid or peony hoops will prevent the stems from falling over.

Recommended

T. argenteum forms a low mat of finely divided silvery-grey foliage. It grows 8–12" tall, spreads 12–18" and bears daisy-like white flowers (Zones 4–7).

T. balsamita (costmary, balsam tansy) is a bold plant, with its larger leaves and small, daisy-like flowers. Its leaves are used for potpourris and sachets, and as "strewing" herbs to repel vermin.

T. coccineum (painted daisy, *Pyrethrum*) is an erect, bushy plant that grows 18–36" tall and spreads 12–18". The main flush of white, pink, purple or red, yellow-centered flowers occurs in early summer, but some flowering will continue until fall. **'Brenda'** has red or magenta flowers. **'James Kelway'** bears scarlet red flowers (Zones 4–9).

T. parthenium (feverfew) is a bushy plant with fern-like foliage. It grows 12–36" tall, spreads 12–24" and bears clusters of small daisy-like flowers. **'Gold Ball'** forms a compact

T. vulgare

Tansy species are native to parts of Europe and Asia. They've managed to naturalize elsewhere in the world, especially in North America, to the point of becoming invasive and weedy.

plant bearing yellow, double flowers. **'Snowball'** bears double, white flowers (Zones 4–9).

T. vulgare (tansy, golden buttons) forms a large, erect, wide-spreading mound. It grows 2–4' tall, spreads 18–36" and bears clusters of bright yellow, button-like flowers mid-summer to fall. **'Crispum'** (curly tansy) is a compact plant with crinkled, lacy foliage. It is less invasive than the species (Zones 3–8).

Harvesting and Processing

Pick the leaves all summer for fresh use. Store dried sprigs whole, in airtight containers, for later use.

Uses

Tansy isn't used for culinary purposes but is still useful. Rubbing the leaves of *T. vulgare* gently into the coat of your dog or cat can prevent fleas. Hang bunches of tansy indoors to deter flies. Place dried sprigs under carpets as a natural deodorizer. Add dried and fresh leaves to sachets used for repelling insects in closets and drawers. Use chopped leaves and flowers to deter ants and mice in areas where they're a problem.

The roots and leaves of *T. vulgare* have been used for making dyes for centuries. Harvest them for this use when fully open and most colorful, and then dry them. Use the roots to make a green dye and the flowers to make golden yellow dyes.

The flowers from any tansy species can be added to potpourri and aromatic sachets.

Do not take tansy internally without being under the supervision of a medical professional. An overdose can be quite harmful, and even fatal.

The brilliant yellow of fresh tansies (above); tansy insect repellant (below)

Tarragon

Artemisia

It's ironic that this plant gets as large as it does when you only need a tiny amount to flavor a dish. Too much tarragon can be overwhelming. That being said, there are many opportunities to use tarragon in your cooking, and you'll still have too much left over in the garden when it's all said and done. Tarragon goes well with poultry and tastes great in chicken salad; it's also refreshing blended with fresh mint and steeped to make tea. Tarragon is one of those herbs that isn't nearly as good alone as it is when blended with the right ingredients.

Tarragon is high in calcium, potassium, vitamin A, thiamine, riboflavin and niacin.

Features
Parts used: leaves
Hardiness: zones 3–7

Growing
Tarragon thrives in **full sun** but grows well in **partial sun**. The soil should be **well drained, light** and **fertile**. Tarragon has to be propagated by cuttings or division. If you find seed, it's the inferior species *A. dracunculoides* or Russian tarragon. Divide in spring. Tarragon benefits from heavy mulching during the winter months to adequately protect the roots. Starter plants can be planted out after the risk of frost has passed.

Tarragon is often used to flavor vinegar.

Tips
Tarragon is suitable for the back or middle of mixed perennial borders. It can also be added to herb gardens and vegetable gardens. Tarragon can also be grown successfully in containers outdoors. Growing tarragon indoors can be more than a little tricky and isn't recommended.

Recommended
A. dracunculus (tarragon, French tarragon) is the better tasting species of the two. It's important not to confuse this species with *A. dracunculoides* (Russian tarragon), which is very bitter and difficult to dry for later use. *A. dracunculus* is a clump-forming

A young *A. dracunculus* plant (above), *A. vulgare* in a pot with marigold, parsley and tarragon (below)

perennial with aromatic, tender narrow leaves that clothe the tall, upright stems from top to bottom. The aroma and flavor of the leaves is reminiscent of anise or licorice. Insignificant, pale yellow flowers are borne in late summer. It grows 3–4' tall and 12–24" wide.

Harvesting and Processing

As hard frost approaches in the fall and the leaves begin to wither, it's good to know that you'll have lots of tarragon for winter stews, soups and meat dishes. Fresh tarragon is more flavorful than dried, but are good in a pinch. Harvest the leaves throughout the growing season for immediate use. For later use, harvest the stems in late summer and strip the leaves from the stems. Chop the leaves finely, add water and pour into ice cube trays for tarragon

Tarragon and mint combine to make a refreshing tea.

cubes. To dry, hang the stems upside down until dry. Strip the leaves from the stems once dry into airtight containers.

Uses

Fresh tarragon can be added to herb butters. It's also a great addition to mint for a refreshing tea. Tarragon is also one of the four essential herbs in the *fines herbes* mixture, exclusive to French cuisine. The warming essence of tarragon is an ideal complement to fish and shellfish. It also works beautifully with fowl, game, egg dishes and casseroles. Fresh leaves can be added to dressings and green salads. When steeped in white vinegar, tarragon imparts a particularly savory flavor. Combing root vegetables like carrots and parsnips with tarragon brings out their natural sweetness. Tarragon is best when only briefly heated, so add it in the last few minutes of cooking.

Crafters have been known to use the essential oils from tarragon in herbal soaps, lotions and bath products.

The species name dracunculus, *is from the Latin meaning "a little dragon," and named for the species' supposed ability to cure the bites of serpents and mad dogs.*

Thyme

Thymus

Thyme is a classic and very well-known herb. It has a timeless quality that lends itself to culinary arts and horticultural uses. This versatile, hardy and tasty herb is a staple in most kitchens. All thyme species are rich in volatile oils that not only complement certain foods, but also scented products such as perfume, toiletries and potpourri. Thyme has also been employed medicinally to treat coughs, flatulence, stomach troubles, asthma and indigestion. There are a wide variety of species, hybrids and cultivars to choose from, and whether you're selecting one or more for a garden path, recipe or craft, you'll have plenty of choice.

Features

Parts used: leaves, in some cases the whole plant or oil
Hardiness: zones 3–9

Growing

Thyme prefers **full sun**. The soil should be **neutral to alkaline** and of **poor to average fertility**. **Good drainage** is essential. It is beneficial to work leaf mould and sharp lime-stone gravel into the soil to improve structure and drainage.

Tips

Creeping selections of thyme are useful for sunny, dry locations at the front of borders, between or beside paving stones, in rock gardens and rock walls and in containers. Taller selections are suitable for the former but also for strawberry or herb pots, mixed herb gardens and hypertufa containers.

Once the plants have finished flowering, shear them back by about half to encourage new growth and prevent the plants from becoming too woody.

Recommended

T. x *citriodorus* (lemon-scented thyme) forms a mound of lemon-scented, dark green foliage. The flowers are pale pink. Cultivars with silver- or gold-margined leaves are available. This hybrid grows 10–12" tall and 24" wide. **'Archer's Gold'** is a compact plant with bright yellow, lemony foliage and pale purple flowers. **'Aureus'** produces pale, gold-green foliage and pink flowers, **'Bertram Anderson'** is a low-growing cultivar with red-tinged tips and golden foliage. **'Golden King'** is an upright cultivar with yellow-edged leaves (Zones 4–9).

'Silver Posie' used as edging

T. herba-barona (caraway thyme) is a delightful, sweet selection that produces leaves that taste like caraway. It is a low-growing plant, well suited to rock gardens. **'Lemon Carpet'** and **'Lemon Scented'** produce lemony tasting leaves and **'Nutmeg'** is also very small in size, producing low-growing, ground-hugging leafy stems. Its leaves taste like nutmeg (Zones 5–9).

T. **'Orange Balsam'** (orange balsam thyme) produces foliage with a potent and tasty orange flavor. It is useful for cooking, teas or for use as a garnish (Zones 5–9).

T. praecox (creeping thyme) is a mat-forming, creeping species with tiny, hairy-fringed leaves and purple flowers. It only grows 2" high but 18" wide (Zones 4–8). **Subsp. *britannicus* 'Lanuginosis'** (*pseudolanuginosus*,

Thyme is an attractive groundcover in perennial beds (above and opposite page).

woolly thyme) is a prostrate, woody perennial or shrublet with hairy stems and tiny, grayish green leaves covered in woolly hairs. It produces pale pink flowers in mid-summer. It grows only 1–3" tall and up to 36" wide (Zones 5–7). **Var. *coccineus*** (red-flowered thyme) produces bright crimson-pink flowers and dark green leaves that turn bronze in fall. **'Elfin'** is a taller cultivar with glossy, rounded leaves and clusters of magenta pink flowers. **'Pink Chintz'** has grey-green, hairy leaves and salmon pink flowers (Zones 3–8).

T. serpyllum (wild thyme, creeping thyme, mother-of-thyme) is another prostrate, creeping species with tiny, hairy leaves and clusters of pink to purple flowers. It grows ½–3" tall and up to 36" wide.

T. vulgaris (common thyme) forms a bushy mound of dark green leaves. The flowers may be purple, pink or white. This species grows 12–18" tall and 24" wide. **'Erectus'** is an upright plant with camphor-scented leaves, growing 6–9" tall. **'Silver Posie'** is the best of the silver thyme selections, bearing white-variegated leaves and pale purple-pink flowers (Zones 3–8).

Harvesting and Processing

Harvest fresh leaves all summer by removing entire stems and stripping them of their leaves; leave them intact if you plan to remove the thyme from the dish before serving, or if using as a garnish. You can also dry the leafy stems for later use. Simply cut the stems from the base of the plant and dry on screens or in paper bags. Once leaves are dry, strip them from the stems and store in air-tight containers. Fresh stems can also be frozen in a layer or two of tin foil and will keep for months. The ice cube method can also be used to store fresh thyme for use through the winter.

Uses

Thyme is a popular culinary herb used to flavor soups, stews, casseroles and with roasts. It is synonymous with meat, fish and most vegetable dishes and one of the main ingredients in a *bouquet garni*. Different types of thyme work well with different dishes. Lemony tasting thyme selections are often best with fish and vegetable dishes, while earthy types are more suited to meat. Spicy selections can be used in just about any dish. Throwing whole, slightly dried leafy stems on the coals of the barbecue will flavor whatever happens to be on the grill. Thyme-infused oils and vinegars are delicious on fresh green salads.

Dried thyme leaves can be added to a variety of handmade items including soaps, lotions, room fresheners and sachets.

Thyme is a member of the mint family.

Flowering thyme in a container (above); thyme in a *bouquet garni* (below)

Vietnamese Coriander

Polygonum

Vietnamese coriander is quite popular in Asian cooking, especially Malaysian, Vietnamese, Thai and Chinese. It's also commonly referred to as mint because of its flavor and aroma, which tastes like a combination of coriander and mint, spicy yet sweet. If you were to travel to Vietnam, you'd find this herb in fresh salads, raw spring rolls and bowls of beef noodles sold piping hot by street vendors. In the Philippines, it is served with fertilized duck eggs; in Malaysian cuisine, it is the essential ingredient of a spicy soup called *laksa*. Vietnamese coriander may not be as popular in American cuisine, but it deserves a place in our diet. It's fresh, tasty, versatile and healthy.

Features
Other names: Vietnamese cilantro, Vietnamese mint, Cambodian mint, hot mint
Parts used: leaves
Hardiness: zones 10–11, perennial that is often grown as an annual

Growing

A location with **afternoon shade** or **filtered shade** all day long is best for this herb, but it can tolerate **full to partial sun. Moist, well drained soil** with **average to high fertility** is preferred. Vietnamese coriander is an understory plant in its native habitat, so a sheltered position will protect its tender leaves from burning.

Tips

Grow Vietnamese coriander outdoors, as an ornamental edging plant in mixed beds and borders because of its low-growing habit and pretty, fragrant leaves. Integrated into a herb or vegetable garden for more practical use. It will also thrive in containers, which will allow you to bring it indoors during winter. It grows vigorously and may outgrow its container quickly.

Recommended

P. odoratum is a low-growing groundcover perennial that produces distinctive narrow, pointed leaves with unique, chestnut-colored markings in the center of some leaves. The stems have a hint of burgundy as contrast to the bright green. It grows approximately 6–12" tall and wide. Flowers are produced but are considered insignificant.

Harvesting and Processing

Pick the leaves throughout the growing season or year-round, if growing the herb indoors. Use fresh because the leaves don't dry well.

Vietnamese coriander with mint and feverfew

If you cannot find a local nursery that sells Vietnamese coriander, try buying the leafy stems at an Asian market. Propagate stems either in water or moist potting soil until rooted. Once rooted, plant in slightly larger pots for use year-round.

Uses

This herb is slightly bitter and spicy. It is often used in place of peppermint or coriander in various dishes. The fresh lettuce-like leaves are tasty in simple chicken and vegetable dishes. They will also lend a unique flavor to sandwiches and soups. Use it fresh and only add it to dishes just before serving.

Vietnamese coriander is said to treat swellings, acne, indigestion, flatulence and stomach pain. It is also said to detoxify food.

Wild Strawberry

Fragaria

Wild strawberry isn't all about the fruit, although it would be criminal to ignore the wonderful berries it produces. The leaves and roots of *F. vesca* are also useful for their medicinal benefits. There are many types of strawberries on the market, all unique in one way or another. The following selections are the originals, species found in their native habitats without any human alteration or interference. They, too, can cultivated in home gardens for their luxurious berries, which can be used in many delicious dishes.

Features
Other names: mountain strawberry, wood strawberry, alpine strawberry
Parts used: fruit, leaves
Hardiness: zones 4–9

Growing

Wild strawberries will grow in **full sun** and will tolerate partial sun but with slightly less fruit production. The soil should be **humus-rich, well drained** and **moist**. Sow seed indoors in late winter or outdoors in late fall. Although perennial, the plants will run their course over a few years and will need to be replaced by new plants, for maximum fruit production.

Tips

Wild strawberries need a lot of room to grow, and the more plants you have, the more fruit you get. They can be successfully grown in the ground or in containers and hanging baskets. Overwinter in a cold garage, or try growing them indoors in direct sun.

Recommended

F. vesca (wild strawberry) produces very long runners (stems that root at the nodes). It bears toothed coarsely textured oval leaves and five-petalled, white flowers with yellow centers. Bright red, tangy but sweet fruits are produced. The plants grow almost 12" tall and up to 8" wide but will spread via runners to form new plants. **'Fructu Albo'** has unusual creamy, white fruits that taste similar to the red fruits of the species. They are said to be less attractive to birds. **'Multiplex'** is an ornamental selection with double flowers and smaller, red fruits. **'Ruegen'** is a very productive selection and will bear fruit in its first year. *F. v. sempiflorans* (alpine strawberry) grows 2–10" tall and 6" wide. It bears leaves and flowers very similar to the species but

Strawberry tea

does not set down runners. It can only be propagated by seed.

Harvesting and Processing

Harvest the leaves in early summer and dry for use in tea and other infusions. To dry, place them on screens or hang in bunches on a drying rack. Pick the fruit when red and ripe, and eat fresh or freeze.

Uses

Include dried or fresh leaves with other herbs in teas; they taste better in a blend rather than on their own.

Eat the berries fresh or cooked into into desserts, jams and preserves, juice, syrup or wine. They can also be added to summer drinks and smoothies.

Medicinally, strawberry leaves are said to treat diarrhea and digestive problems when eaten. Externally, the leaves help to heal skin problems and blemishes, sunburn and stained teeth. The leaves can be made into a mouthwash to soothe mouth ulcers, cankers and sore gums.

Glossary

Acid soil: soil with a pH lower than 7.0

Alkaline soil: soil with a pH higher than 7.0

Analgesic: a pain-relieving substance

Annual: a plant that germinates, flowers, sets seeds and dies in one growing season

Apothecary: an old-fashioned term for a person who prepared and dispensed drugs to the sick

Basal leaves: leaves that form from the crown, at the base of the plant

Bolting: when a plant produces flowers and seeds prematurely

Bract: a special, modified leaf located at the base of a flower or inflorescence; bracts may be small or large, green or colored

Crown: the part of the plant at or just below soil level where the shoots join the roots

Cultivar: a cultivated plant variety with one or more distinct differences from the species, e.g., in flower color or disease resistance

Deadhead: removing spent flowers to maintain a neat appearance and encourage a long blooming season

Decoction: the extract of hard or woody herb material (e.g., roots, bark, nuts, seeds) obtained by simmering the material in boiling water for about 30 minutes and straining while still hot

Direct sow: to sow seeds directly into the garden

Dormancy: a period of plant inactivity, usually during winter or unfavorable conditions

Double flower: a flower with an unusually large number of petals

Essential oil: a volatile oil, extracted by distilling a plant, that usually has the characteristic aroma of the source plant

Genus: a category of biological classification between the species and family levels; the first word in a scientific name indicates the genus

Hardy: capable of surviving unfavorable conditions, such as cold weather or frost, without protection

Humus: decomposed or decomposing organic material in the soil

Hybrid: a plant resulting from natural or human-induced cross-breeding between varieties, species or genera

Ice cube method: a way to preserve fresh herbs (mainly their flowers and leaves) by mixing them with water and freezing them into ice cubes; sometimes the herb is left whole and other times it is chopped before being frozen

Inflorescence: an arrangement of flowers on a single stem

Infusion: a liquid obtained by pouring boiling water over soft herb parts (leaves or petals) and letting them steep for 10 to 15 minutes before straining

Invasive: able to spread aggressively from the planting site and outcompete others

Loam: a loose soil composed of clay, sand and organic matter, often highly fertile

Mordant: a substance used to fix dyes when applied to the fabric being dyed

Mulch: a material, (e.g., shredded bark, pine cones, leaves, straw), used to surround a plant to protect it from weeds, cold or heat and to promote moisture retention

Perennial: a plant that takes three or more years to complete its life cycle

Plantlet: a young or small plant

pH: a measure of acidity or alkalinity; soil pH influences availability of nutrients for plants

Rhizome: a root-like, food-storing stem that grows horizontally at or just below soil level, from which new shoots may emerge

Rosette: a low, flat cluster of leaves arranged like the petals of a rose

Salve: a soothing ointment

Seedhead: dried, inedible fruit that contains seeds

Self-seeding: reproducing by means of seeds without human assistance, so that new plants constantly replace those that die

Single flower: a flower with a single ring of typically four or five petals

Slow oven: an oven set at a temperature of 300° F

Spathe: a leaf-like bract that encloses a flower cluster or spike

Species: the fundamental unit of biological classification; the entity from which cultivars and varieties are derived

Standard: a tree or shrub pruned to form a rounded head of branches at the top of a clearly visible stem

Strewing herbs: plants with aromatic flowers, foliage or potent oils that were used to scent clothing, or inside houses to mask odors or to repel insects during the Middle Ages; examples include basil, lemon balm, lavender and tansy

Tender: incapable of surviving the climatic conditions of a given region and requiring protection from frost or cold

Tincture: a solution extracted from plant material that has been crushed in an alcohol or alcohol-water solution

Tisane: a tea-like, medicinal drink made by pouring boiling water onto fresh or dried but unfermented plant material; sometimes also made with barley

Umbel: flowers on stalks, radiating in a U shape from a single point at the top of a stem, e.g., dill flowers

Understory plant: a plant that prefers to grow beneath the canopies of trees in a woodland setting

Variegation: foliage that has more than one color, often patched, striped or bearing leaf margins of a different color

Variety: a naturally occurring variant of a species

Index of Plant Names

Boldface type refers to the primary species accounts; *italics* indicate botanical names.